BUSINESS/SCIENCE/TECHNOLOGY
DIVISION

The Chicago Pub

Received

BUSINESS/SCIENCE/TECHNOLOGY
DIVISION

GOLDEN KNIGHTS

The History
of the U.S. Army
Parachute Team

R.C. MURRAY

DARING BOOKS

CANTON • OHIO

End sheet art work by Golden Knight Bill Jackson.
(This is a limited edition print and is not for sale. It was a gift to the Knights from the artist.)

Book and Cover Design
Mary Miller • Rich Hendrus • Dennis Bartow

The following people contributed the photographs in this book: **Bob Turner, Don Kidd, Joe Gonzalez, Gary Winkler, John R. Spann, Brynn McCleod, Chuck Roberts, Jake Brown, Ken Kassens, Kevin Peyton, Todd Lorenzo, Tom Shriver, Kevin Oleksy, Joe Belcher, Laurel Perry, R.C. Murray, Dennis Bartow, Mary Miller,** and numerous unknown team members/photographers who documented team history with their cameras.

Published by Daring Books
P.O. Box 20050GK, Canton, Ohio 44701
(216) 454-7519

Daring Publishing Group offers special discounts for bulk purchases of its products to be used for fund-raising, premium gifts, sales promotions, educational use, etc. Book excerpts or special editions can be produced to specification. For information contact the **Special Sales Department, Daring Publishing Group, 913 W. Tuscarawas St., Canton, Ohio 44702. Or call 1-800-445-6321.**

Library of Congress Cataloging-in-Publication Data

Murray, R. C., 1955-
   Golden Knights : the history of the U.S. Army Parachute Team / by R.C. Murray.
      p.   cm.
     Includes index.
     ISBN 0-938936-96-4
     1. United States. Army. Parachute Team--History.
  2. Skydiving--United States--History.   I. Title.
UD483.M87 1990
356'.1663'0973--dc20   90-37169
                          CIP

10 9 8 7 6 5 4 3 2 1

Printed in the United States of America.

Dedication

THIS BOOK IS DEDICATED TO
Brigadier General Joseph Stilwell, Jr.
The Father of the U.S. Army Parachute Team

ACKNOWLEDGMENTS

Long, neat rows of sweet corn and sugar cane crossed the horizon of a golden sunset. It could have been tobacco or cotton, I suppose, but it was my dream and I liked sweet corn and sugar cane. Besides, I'd had "The Dream" often enough—it seemed by now I controlled The Dream even in my subconscious. My friends and I were flying, or I should say floating. I was falling back to earth but less aware of my descent than I was of my forward movement over the dark green countryside.

The Dream had been with me as long as I could remember. It was part of me now. Quite often I'd heard grownups talk of so-called nightmares about falling. These folks would say things like, "If you don't wake up from a dream like that, they say you'll die."

But who were the "they" who said such things and where did they get their information? They never asked me. I slept right through my dreams, and I woke up feeling just fine. Sometimes I dreamed I landed next to one of the more fishable-looking ponds I'd spotted from above and set about checking it out. My dreams never malfunctioned. The days following "The Dream" were always joyful. I was motivated, exhilarated even. To my young mind, I'd been like the angels in my dream, capable of flight. The Lord and I both knew I was far from being angelic! But I had flown. Really flown! And I loved it.

The Dream started coming to me less often beginning in January 1974, after the Army stood me in the door of a C-130. The altitude was low—only 1,250 feet, but the Georgia/ Alabama countryside was beautiful just the same.

"Scared?" the jumpmaster asked, grinning like a possum after giving us the *One Minute Warning*.

I just shook my head and wondered why he'd ask such a silly question. All my life I'd dreamed of being here. My only disappointment was not being able to find the sweet corn and sugar cane. After all, it was January. I had another disappointment, too. The ride down was entirely too short. I needed more altitude.

Sixteen years later I sat in the door of a Blackhawk helicopter looking at the Carolina countryside. It, too, conjured up memories of The Dream, which by now was indeed a memory. This time the altitude was slightly higher and I'd soon be free of the umbilical cord that had prevented me from experiencing the "free" in freefall. I would at last live The Dream of my youth to its fullest. I even spotted a few fishable-looking ponds that I would have dropped in on had my instructors been so accommodating. Although I didn't have quite the control I came to have over The Dream (there still wasn't any sweet corn around), I was trained well by my instructors and therefore prepared for any emergency.

Their timely instruction was a fitting end for a book project which I sometimes wondered if I would ever complete. Thanks Fred, J.B., Willie, Jay, Gene, Belkis and, of course, Mark. You don't know how much I appreciate you and the entire 82d SPC.

Thanks especially to my wife, Gloria, who was a writer's widow for 6 to 8 hours every evening, for weeks at a time as I struggled to turn piles of notes into a manuscript; and thank you, Shelly and Patrick, for giving daddy peace and quite to write!

I also want to thank all my teammates for accepting me onto the team and for trusting me to tell your story. To my staff—Tom Shriver, Kevin Oleksy and Joe Belcher—thanks for helping me sort and select the photos used in this book and a special thanks for enduring my mood swings as my self-imposed deadline neared. You know the guidelines I set for myself, agreeing to write the book on my own time at home. If I lost my temper at any time for lack of sleep, I apologize. If I remembered to make you feel appreciated,

good. It's because you were.

Laura Wilson, Laurel Perry and Donna Council—although you weren't with me when the book was being written, you stood by me as I nervously awaited its publication. Thank you for your support, ladies.

Thanks to all team photographers, past and present, with a special thanks to K.C. Kassens, Kevin Peyton and Chuck Roberts. The Army Parachute Team is fueled by publicity and the photographs you've provided this team have kept it on the road for a number of years.

Jim Perry, John Hollis, Spider Wrenn, Don Kidd, Phil Miller—I could go on and on, but I won't. I don't want to start another book just yet! I just want you all to know the time you gave to me in interviews, in lending me personal photos and news clippings, in simply talking with me as opposed to talking to me—I thank you from the bottom of my heart. Every one of you inspired me to drive on when the project bogged down in the red tape mire.

I couldn't possibly mention each outstanding member of the Golden Knights, past and present—space just will not permit. I simply tried to give a good, representative sampling of the excellent team members who have comprised America's Golden Knights. My apologies to those of you who may be unsung heroes of this book; however, you do have the personal satisfaction of knowing that you have made hundreds of thousands of Americans proud over the years! That is the purpose of this book: to record for posterity the courage, discipline and dedication of the men and women of the Golden Knights!

Lastly, as I look over this manuscript, the result of many months research and writing, I have to say thank you to Dave Goldie and Bob Finn, without whom this book would never have been written. It was you who brought me to this team and asked me to write. You allowed me to do what no one else would and I thank you.

R.C. MURRAY

TABLE OF CONTENTS

FOREWORD...................................9

PART 1
   A HOMECOMING.....................13

PART 2
   HISTORY IN THE MAKING...........39

PART 3
   REAL PEOPLE, REAL SOLDIERS—REAL HEROES......129

PART 4
   A GOLDEN FUTURE 207

ABOUT THE AUTHOR..................220

INDEX 221

GLOSSARY.........................224

FOREWORD

by
Captain James M. Perry
AUS (Retired)

It has a prelude, this little story of how the Army Parachute Team, "The Golden Knights," was born.

We were in a "Huey" at 15,000 feet over Normandy drop zone, rotors clamoring to keep the little ship and its six passengers in the turbulent air. We were in a hail storm, most of it beating at the face of Joe Stilwell as he sat on the floor, feet on the skids, squinting through the foul weather at the DZ far below.

"Gim'me a right ten!" he yelled to the pilot, clenching his fist twice. He thumbed in the direction of the stand of pine trees on the far side. The co-pilot looked at me quizzically and I shook my head no. The Huey continued on.

I leaned over the General's shoulder, clutching at his parachute harness, fearful we'd over-run the release point. Joe wasn't the best spotter in the business. It was also his first delay jump from that altitude—a new and terrifying experience for any neophyte.

"We got'ta go, Joe!" I yelled in his ear, "If you don't make it now, we're gon'na miss the DZ!"

"No...!" he yelled back, "...right! Right five more!"

"Get out, General!" I pointed down at the ground fleeting by.

"You mean...now?" he said, almost as a child asking permission.

It looked close enough that we could all make the DZ. I nodded. He'd

go now but only because I'd told him it was okay to do that.

But I was too late.

Someone put their feet in Joe's back and shoved hard. Not with disrespect, but more to say, "...hey, you're gon'na play on this team, you got'ta give the rest of us a chance to jump, too!"

Two years earlier, those of us from Operation "White Star," Laos, 1959-60, had just returned from a new and burgeoning war in Southeast Asia. I was a detachment commander in Special Forces, Fort Bragg and it would be a year before they'd call us Green Berets.

There were no more after-action reports to write; no more debriefings to attend. Those who were free of duties were entitled to a leave and I enjoyed mine at my family quarters in Corrigidor Courts, the base. There were only a few days of that before I received a phone call from HQs, XVIII Airborne Corps, telling me to report to General Stilwell, then the Chief of Staff.

"Fatigues are fine, Captain," the aide said.

As far as decorations are concerned, there's no place on the fatigue uniform to display more than your CIB and parachute badge. If I had to face a General, I'd prefer to do it with ribbons, but I dressed in fatigues and put on my best jump boots—the Corcorans. On any work day at Fort Bragg, I was as natty as the rest.

He kept me waiting in the outer office for more than a half-hour. I drank two cups of coffee and smoked several cigarettes. I tried to concentrate on a magazine that recapped the mini-war in Indo-China from which we'd just returned. The aide, a captain younger than I, was strangely silent. He never said why the General wanted to see me.

Joe Stilwell was a pensive, stern-faced man with close-cropped salt-and-pepper hair. He had only a faint hint of his famous father's appearance, "Vinegar Joe." He smiled rarely and when he did it was genuine. But when he was with parachute friends, he was effervescent. He seemed that way today.

"You care for a cup of coffee?" he asked.

"Thank you, Sir."

Coffee cups in a General's office are petite, fragile. I was accustomed to a larger mug and another cup couldn't hurt me.

"I understand you're a skydiver," he said finally.

"I'm a delay-fall jumper, yes." I told him.

"What's the difference?"

I shrugged. There wasn't any real difference except that I had learned free-fall parachuting in the late 'Forties, the old tuck-and-tumble method.

"Skydiving" carried the connotation that it was nothing more than a high, prolonged swan dive. Something exceedingly safe, like leaving the board and never reaching the water.

"I don't like the expression," I said.

"What's wrong with the word 'skydiving'?" he growled. I was certain I'd said the wrong thing.

"It's too corny. Makes it sound like something easy to do."

"Isn't it?"

"No," I said, "...no it isn't. It's a dangerous game, Sir."

"We're not having any trouble with it here."

That was true. Several sport parachute clubs had been in operation on base for over a year. No one had been killed yet and the few broken bones we'd had were normal at any airborne training base.

"It takes time—a lot of time—and a hell of a lot of jumps to learn stable delay, Sir," I told him. "People are being conned by hype that it's the safest sport in the world. We've been lucky here at Bragg. We could have a fatality any day,'' I added.

When he was contemplative, Joe Stilwell always turned his chair away, looked out the window, his fingertips folded. He did that now, his questions directed at me over his shoulder.

''Do you think you could...say...teach me the French Cross?''

He was speaking of the body position used in the late 'Fifties for maintaining a stable face-to-earth attitude during free-fall. The moments when a parachutist is, literally, free as a bird.

So that's what he wants.

''You bet, Sir,'' I grinned. ''It's easy.''

''Show me,'' he said.

He rose abruptly, moved to the front of his desk and plopped, face down, on the carpet. He spread his arms and legs and arched his back. I sat for a moment, stunned a little that a Brigadier General in the United States Army would be so earthy.

''Well...?'' he said, arching harder and spreading his legs even more, ''...show me.''

We spent the next few minutes together, he the student, as I corrected his body position a little and explained the importance of arching his back. When we'd finished, he jumped to his feet and dusted off his hands.

''How'd you like to command the United States Army Parachute Team?'' he asked when he settled in his chair again.

''I didn't know we had one,'' I said.

''We don't,'' he grinned, ''but we're going to.'' Stilwell contemplated the thought. He reversed his chair and looked out the window again, curling his fingertips once more.

''It's going to be a lot of hard work,'' he said over his shoulder. He spun back to face me and signed a paper in front of him, my orders, handing it to me. It was not expected that I should read it. I folded it in my left hand and remained at

quasi-attention.

I saluted. ''I'll try my best, General.''

''Don't just try, Jim.'' He grinned and shook hands to cinch the deal. ''Let's do it.''

And so we did.

11

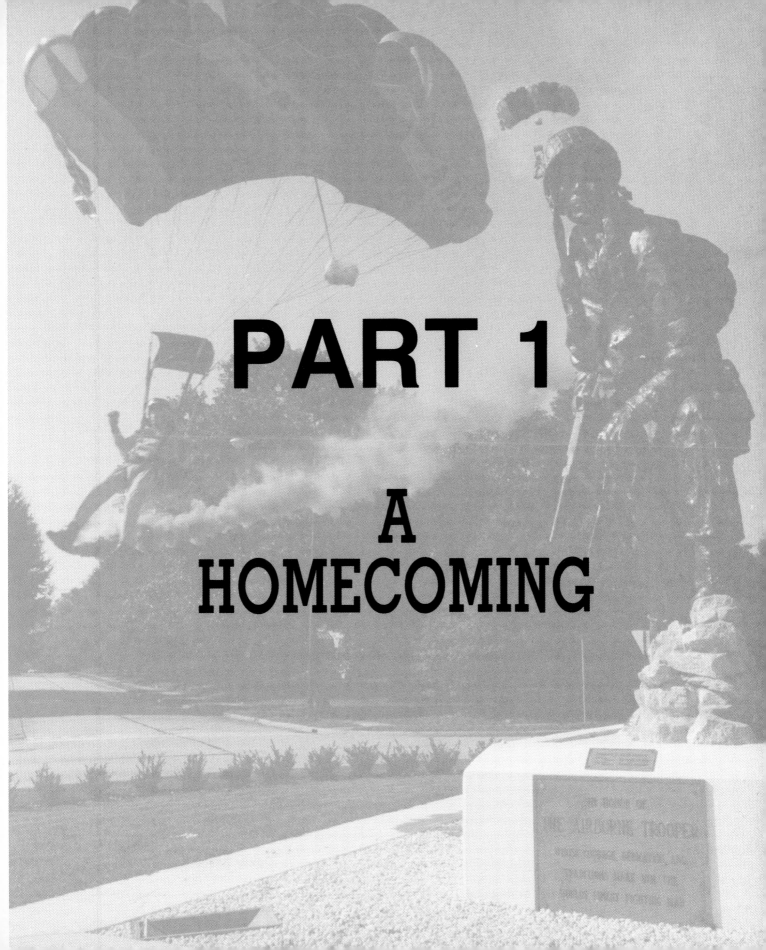

PART 1

A
HOMECOMING

PART 1

A
HOMECOMING

U.S. Parachute Team, 1961.

Then Sen. Hubert Humphrey tries on Jim Perry's jump helmet following a VIP demo early in 1960 when the team was "playing politics" to get official recognition by the Department of the Army.

Early STRAC Sports Parachute Team displaying team's initial contribution to its trophy room. Brigadier General Joe Stilwell back center.

(Kneeling l to r) Master Sergeant John T. Hollis, 1st Sergeant; 1st Lieutenant Roy D. Martin, Executive Officer; Captain James M. Perry, Commanding Officer; 1st Lieutenant James P. Pearson, Operations Officer; 2nd Lieutenant Douglas C. Rummels, Public Relations Officer; Specialist Fourth Class Bobby W. Letbetter; (Standing l to r) Sergeant Danny Byard, Private First Class Leroy K. Smith, Sergeant Loy B. Brydon, Sergeant Wilfred J. A. Charette, Sergeant First Class Harold R. Lewis, Sergeant Joe E. Norman, Specialist Fifth Class Richard T. Fortenberry, Private First Class Robert J. McDonnell, Specialist Fourth Class Coy O. McDonald, Sergeant First Class William E. Edge, Jr., Sergeant First Class Gerald F. Bourquin, Sergeant Ralph K. Palmer and Private First Class Keith C. Jorgenson.

"Look, Daddy!" A small boy tugs on his father's sleeve and points to a circling twin-engine plane. A crowd gathers, anticipating the event about to occur as the distinctive black and gold craft ascends to jump altitude. The words U.S. ARMY are proudly painted in gold on its left wing.

A young man in glistening black sweats stands nearby, in communication with the plane by handset. He raises a wind sock and unfolds a flourescent-orange, x-shaped target which he places on the ground, in a roped-off corner of a shopping mall parking lot.

Inside the airplane, eleven soldiers snap up and strap on equipment, all of which is black: glossy boots, jumpsuit, parachute, gloves and a padded leather cap. Only a small golden patch on the front of their jumpsuits and back of their parachutes identifies this mysterious-looking band of dark-clad soldiers.

They're members of the U.S. Army

Parachute Team, better known as the "Golden Knights." And in just a moment, they'll demonstrate to the crowd gathered below why they're called "knights" and how they've earned a "golden" reputation.

The co-pilot shouts something to the crew chief above the roar of the engines and wind from the open cargo doors near the rear of the aircraft. The crew chief passes the message via hand-signal to the team leader. The signal— hands crossed at the wrists forming an X, tells them they have a "hot target" 12,500 feet below.

Moments later, the jumper selected to jump with the American flag and narrate today's special press show makes his way to the left cargo door. He pauses only a second to speak to a shivering news reporter who's bundled up in an oversized-jumpsuit she borrowed from another jumper. She hadn't believed him when he

Stack-out exit from F27 Fokker.

16

warned her about the temperature difference "at altitude," a difference of four degrees for every 1,000 feet. He gives her a wink and a smile, turns and faces the front of the plane, then exits the aircraft by sidestepping through the door—arms and legs outstretched, back arched.

As he leaves the plane, he tugs on a lanyard attached to a metal bracket on his boot. Two smoke canisters begin leaving a trail of red smoke as he returns to earth at terminal velocity—120 mph. At 2,500 feet he deploys his parachute, its rectangular-shaped or "square" canopy also denoting the team's black and gold colors.

At 1,500 feet he unfurls Old Glory from one of his suspension lines, and those spectators who were sitting, rise to the strains of our National Anthem playing from unseen loudspeakers. All eyes follow the jumper and the flag. Children place little hands over big hearts. Weathered old men make themselves stand tall and salute their flag, many remembering years past when they, too, served with honor.

As the last note echoes across the now deathly silent shopping area, the jumper lands softly on the X-shaped target. The unidentified young man in black sweats (actually a teammate serving as ground control) catches the American flag and assists the jumper in taking off his parachute.

Once he's free of his harness, the flag jumper takes up a microphone, introduces himself as Sergeant—always "sergeant," denoting his rank and professionalism. The narrator then describes each maneuver performed by his teammates, while they're being performed.

Two jumpers exit the aircraft simultaneously as evidenced by twin trails of smoke. They "fly" together in freefall simply by moving their arms, legs and body position until they link hand and hand. As they

Perry JMPI's (Jumpmasters Parachute Inspection) Fort Bragg Chief-Of-Staff, Brigadier General Joseph W. Stilwell, Jr.

spiral downward together, one jumper passes a 14-inch wooden baton to the other jumper. Later, that baton will be presented to someone at the show site. With the baton pass completed, each jumper deploys his parachute, then takes his turn landing on the X-shaped target amid cheers and applause from an appreciative audience.

Another jumper leaves the plane, as indicated by a lone trail of smoke. He deploys a round-shaped canopy; next, to demonstrate what a jumper would do for emergency procedures, he deliberately causes his canopy to collapse by releasing one of his risers attached to the parachute harness. As his rate of descent increases rapidly, he releases the other risers, thus "cutting away" the disabled parachute. He returns into freefall and deploys a square canopy, then guides the spare parachute onto the target, as the audience applauds with relief from the tense moments.

Two more jumpers exit the aircraft, trying to achieve as much horizontal separation as possible while in free-fall. After several seconds, they turn and "track" directly back at each other, passing within feet—sometimes inches—of each other. The paths their smoke leaves create a giant, red diamond in the sky. Then, like their teammates before them, with the "diamond track" maneuver completed, they shoot for a dead-center landing.

The five remaining jumpers leave the aircraft. Four of them, with smoke trailing, come together to form a diamond-shaped formation. The fifth jumper, a freefall photographer with a still and a video camera mounted on a light-weight helmet, sticks to the outside of the formation filming their arrival at Anytown, U.S.A. On a signal by the team leader, the four points of the diamond burst apart to the four points of the compass, their smoke trails giving the appearance

Clifford L. Roberts.

963, U.S.A.P.T. Demonstration "Black & Gold" teams.

The baton pass in mid-air.

of an explosion in mid-air.

When all chutes are deployed, three jumpers come together to demonstrate canopy relative work, or CRW (pronounced "crew"). A jumper stacks his canopy atop of another by locking his feet into the suspension lines of the lower jumper, then sliding down to where he is nearly standing on the other jumper's shoulders.

This 3-stack formation breaks off as the lower jumper's feet touch the target, thus landing One, Two, Three. With all jumpers on the ground, the narrator introduces them in a line-up, beginning with the baton pass jumpers and ending with the team leader. As they snap to attention on cue, the little boy who first spotted their plane begins tugging on his father's sleeve.

"Daddy, I wanna do that some day," he tells his father. "Can I go talk to them? Can I?"

Men, women and other children rush out to meet the Golden

Knights and welcome them "home." Next week, these ambassadors of the Army will be performing in another town, probably in another state. To those who meet them, they represent all the sons and daughters who serve this country with pride and professionalism. As such, their performance here is viewed as a homecoming, as well as a demonstration of unequaled aerobatic skill.

ENLISTED REPRESENTATIVES

Since its inception in 1959 as the STRAC (Strategic Army Corps) Parachute Team, the U.S. Army Parachute Team has performed in all 50 states and 42 foreign countries for an audience totaling well over 240 million, or roughly the population of the United States. In addition to aerial demonstrations, Golden Knights compete in national and international parachute competitions, having won more medals, trophies and titles than any other

Staff Sergeant Ray Duffy, the 1965 National Champion and Golden Knights competition team leader, presents a wooden baton passed in mid-air by his team to Sergeant Major of the Army George W. Dunaway.

Bob McDonnell (right center) is welcomed by his teammates at the 6th World Championships held in Orange, Mass, in 1962. McDonnell, who was burned over most of his body in the '61 airplane crash in Wilmington, N.C., joined his teammates for the first time since the crash to cheer them to victory.

Altitude chamber.

Captain Charles L. Mullins, Team Leader 1964, U.S. National Men and Women's Teams, also Executive Officer, U.S.A.P.T.

parachute team in the world—military or civilian.

Comparable to the Air Force's Thunderbirds and the Navy's Blue Angels, the Golden Knights are a Department of Defense-sponsored aerial demonstration team. Unlike the Thunderbirds and Blue Angels, whose star players are pilots and thus officers, the Army Parachute Team is made up of, and run by enlisted soldiers, non-commissioned officers whose whole mission is to "make it happen." The few officer positions on the team allow officers to command, administrate and pilot the aircraft in support of the NCO's who make up the demonstration and competition teams. So, whereas the other demonstration teams are made up of exceptional officers supported by some of the finest enlisted soldiers in the Air Force and Navy, the Army Parachute Team is made up of first-rate enlisted soldiers supported by some of the finest officers in the

Army.

As a unit, the Army Parachute Team consists of 84 men and women who make up six sections: two demonstration teams—the Black and Gold Teams; two competition teams—the Style & Accuracy and Relative Work Teams; an aviation section and a headquarters section. The headquarters and aviation section work together to support the mission of the demonstration and competition teams—from flying and maintaining the team's four airplanes, to providing logistic and administrative support.

Because it's basically an enlisted soldier's team, the Golden Knights represent a thorough cross-section of this country, rather than those who were privileged to attend the U.S. Military Academy at West Point, or who obtained commissions by other diverse means, nearly all of which require a college education or some other specialized training.

Today the Army prides itself on having

Jim Arrender, now a civilian, takes the number 1 spot while Spec. Five Dick Fortenberry takes third overall at the 6th world Championships.

Jim Lewis.

the greatest number of high school graduates in its 215-year history. And yet, the men and women who wear the "black and gold" of the Golden Knights have gone beyond achieving the basics of a good education. They embody the Army's challenge of being "all you can be" by representing the finest soldiers in the Army and the finest precision freefall parachutists in the world.

Sergeants Kevin Breaux of the Knights' Style & Accuracy Team and **Elisa Feldt** of the Knights' Gold Demonstration Team typify Smalltown, U.S.A. and America's rural heritage.

Breaux, a silver medalist at the 1989 U.S. National Skydiving Championships at Muskogee, Oklahoma and 5-year member of the Golden Knights, has never forgotten his humble beginnings in Abbeville, Louisiana. He enlisted in the Army in 1982 as an airborne armor crewman, but being a tanker wasn't enough for him.

"I'd seen a parachute demonstration by the Golden Knights at my high school just before graduation," he explained with a soft-spoken drawl. "After I joined the Army, I started skydiving with the XVIII Airborne Corps Sport Parachute Club (at Fort Bragg, North Carolina). When I had enough jumps (150 freefalls), I tried out for the Golden Knights and made the team."

Breaux began his new assignment as a parachute demonstrator, traveling up to 280 days a year to perform in air shows around the country. Despite his constant absences, however, he says his wife, Stacey, and their two children, Ryan and Heather, remain his impetus and inspiration. He says his proudest moment as a Golden Knight occurred when he performed for his former high school only three years after seeing a Golden Knight demonstration there as a student.

Admitting she was something of a tomboy, Elisa Feldt says she

Staff Sergeant Bill Knight gathers the suspension lines on his parachute after making a perfect dead center landing during the team accuracy event at the 4th CISM (Counseil Internationale du Sport Militare) Parachute Meet held in Eichelberg, West Germany, July 1970.

The first U.S. CISM Parachute Team, 1964: front row, left to right, Captain Roy Martin (Golden Knights Commander), Sergeant First Class Phil Miller (judge), Captain Petric (pilot); back row, left to right, Sergeants Jim Lewis, Ray Duffy, Bobby Letbetter, Dick Harman, Joe Norman and Chuck Hornsby.

The British Parachute Team, the Red Devils, pause for a photo after losing terribly to the Golden Knights in a basketball game. Before that game, however, the Red Devils slaughtered the Knights in a soccer game. Sports have a way of transcending national boundaries.

Sergeant Kevin Breaux

Staff Sergeant John Luke

grew up on a farm near Carpenter, Iowa with no brothers to help with the family chores. Blushing just a bit, this administrative specialist recalls climbing trees as a young girl and even boasts of having a tree fort "way out in the woods."

"I've always liked sports of all kinds," she said. "I especially like outdoor sports, sports which offer adventure, take some effort and present a challenge such as snow skiing, water skiing and rappelling....Yeah, and skydiving, too."

Feldt says she sees no reason to look upon skydiving as a male sport. Admitting that women were probably left out of the sport years ago when the equipment was bulky and heavy, she proved she could hold her own with her male teammates when she was selected for the team in 1988. And although spectators sometimes display their surprise after she lands and removes her padded leather cap, revealing her gender, she says she's living proof that anyone can make giant achievements in the Army.

Staff Sergeants Charlie Brown of the Knights' Relative Work Team and **John Luke** of the Knights' Black Demonstration Team know how it feels to be a nameless face in the crowd, both having grown up in big cities. And yet, they rose above anonymity by earning their identities as Golden Knights.

The only thing the Knights' Charlie Brown might possibly have in common with his comic strip namesake is a slightly cynical sense of humor. He is by no means a loser. In fact, he's a two-time world champion.

A native of Richmond, Va., Brown started skydiving during his senior year at Thomas Jefferson High School. Admitting that he started skydiving only as a hobby, he eventually decided he wanted to make his hobby his occupation. But the only way he could "jump for a

Golden Knights and Thunderbirds.

living'' was through the Army, so he enlisted as a parachute rigger, with long range plans of becoming a Golden Knight.

"We're sponsored by a pretty big company," he explained, grinning boyishly. "I'm doing what I enjoy doing most, and I'm doing it with a group of totally professional soldiers."

With three national and two world championships behind him, Brown will soon be leaving the Army Parachute Team for warrant officer flight school. Unlike the comic strip character who suffers an identity crisis (among other ailments), this Charlie Brown knows who he is and what he wants to do with his life. And he's doing it!

John Luke grew up in the Navy, then joined the Army. But it wasn't as if his father—a Navy captain, had no clues about his son's intended break with family tradition. Although Luke was most familiar with Navy life in and around San Diego, Calif., his father was greatly responsible for influencing his decision to join the Army.

"When I was about 8 years old," Luke said, his dark eyes smiling, "My dad brought home an autographed poster of the Golden Knights. I was enthused about parachuting anyway. I started skydiving while still in high school, then joined the Army so I could continue to jump. At the time, I never dreamed I'd be a Golden Knight one day."

Luke enlisted as an airborne mortar crewman and following initial training, was assigned to The Home of the Airborne—Fort Bragg, North Carolina and the 82d Airborne Division. A year later, he was assigned to another airborne unit, this time in Italy. But his stay there was to be shortened.

In 1985 he was allowed to return to Fort Bragg to try out for the Golden Knights. He returned to Italy only long enough to clear his old unit. Now with four years on the team, Luke continues to jump with unequaled enthusiasm. In August 1989, he even had the opportunity to return home to San Diego and jump for the hometown folks and "show the Navy what the Army's all about!"

From mid-March each year to late November, the Knights' two demonstration teams tour the country, promoting the image of the Army, which in turn, assists in recruiting. As such, the Golden Knights, like their counterparts, the Thunderbirds and Blue Angels, are a recruiting tool.

In addition to aerial demonstration and parachute competitions, Golden Knights annually make hundreds of visits to schools and hospitals, as well as civic and social organizations to promote goodwill and a better understanding of today's Army. These "roving ambassadors of the Army" assure the American public it is well-defended by professional soldiers, all the while inspiring a new generation of Americans to serve this country and a few, a special few, to some day become Golden Knights themselves.

PROFESSIONALS

"They were like the New York Yankees of skydiving," said **Staff Sergeant Jim Coffman**, as he struggled for words to explain his "if ya can't beat 'em, join 'em" attitude toward the Golden Knights.

During the 1981 U.S. National Skydiving Championships in Muskogee, Oklahoma, Coffman was so impressed with the Knights' 4-way Relative Work Team, he decided to give up a welding & repair shop back home in Williamsport, Maryland and enlist in the Army.

Then **Staff Sergeant**, now **Captain Glenn Bangs**; **Specialist Five**, now **Sergeant First Class Andy Gerber**; and **Specialist Five**, now **Sergeant First Class** (retired) **Bob Finn** were part of that 4-way team which so inspired Coffman. They won the nationals that year and went on to win the world championship as well. Coffman says their unbeatable performance in 1981 made him want to be a Golden Knight, to compete as a Golden Knight and to win as a Golden Knight. Of course, he had to join the Army first!

In 1987 Coffman joined Gerber as part of the Knights' 8-way Relative Work Team which beat out intercontinental contenders for the world title in Brazil. A year later, he, Gerber, Bangs and Finn joined **Charlie Brown, Sergeant First Class Chris Wagner** and **Sergeant Willie Lee**, who were also part of that 1987 world championship team, along with **Sergeant Chuck Lackey**—the 1988 U.S. National Accuracy champion, for an exhibition jump into the 1988 Summer Olympics in Seoul, South Korea.

During the 1989 U.S. Nationals, Coffman was the team captain of the Knights' 4-way team which captured the gold medal, finally realizing

the goal he'd been after for nearly a decade. As expected, the Knights successfully defended their 8-way title and they picked up seven of nine possible medals in the Style & Accuracy competition, including finishing first, second and third place overall. Later that summer, they successfully defended their world title in the 8-way relative work event.

The Golden Knights' two competition teams—the Style & Accuracy Team and Relative Work Team, are referred to by many in the sport of parachuting as the best of the best. As surely as every soldier doesn't get to become a Golden Knight, not every Golden Knight gets to become a world champion. But according to **First Sergeant Jeff Moon**, what actually separates competitors from demonstrators is not simply a matter of skill.

"You have demonstrators who simply enjoy the roar and attention of the

crowds and competitors who enjoy the thrill of competition," Moon said. "Nearly all the competitors are former demonstrators who wanted to prove to themselves—if to no one else—they're world class parachutists."

Moon is especially qualified to compare demonstrators and competitors, having performed in aerial demonstrations and having served as a judge during the 1988 and 1989 U.S. Nationals. But his dual qualifications aren't that unusual. Former team member, **Phillip C. Miller**, now a retired major, served as a demonstrator, competitor and judge. In fact, Miller was competition director of the XI World Championships in 1962 and one of the originators of the Federation Aeronautique Internationale (FAI) 5x5 scoring system developed in 1965. In those days, parachute competition was limited to style and accuracy. Relative work or RW competition didn't come along until the mid-70's.

Relative Work, as the name of the competition implies, is genuine work. And yet, some parachutists—particularly the Knights, make it look so simple, spectators watching from the ground might think they could do it with little or no special training. What the eyes see from the ground, however, is only a telescoped picture of what actually occurs in the air:

Eight red, white and blue jumpsuits silhouetted themselves against a gray Spanish sky during freefall from 11,000 feet, all the while assuming ever-changing shapes that look like diagrams of DNA molecules. The more of these molecular formations they complete before reaching break-off altitude (4,000 feet), the greater their chances of beating the Soviet and French teams and winning yet another world title. Relative work requires teamwork and Americans, though notorious individualists, will always work together as a team to achieve a common goal. Since the 8-way

Relative Work event became a world class event in 1975, the Americans have always won. In 1989, America's Golden Knights returned from Spain as the reigning 8-way champions once again.

Accuracy competition is more simple. All the jumper has to do is leave the aircraft at 2,500 feet and land with his or her heel centered squarely on a five centimeter disk (roughly the size of a silver dollar) in the middle of a gravel pit. Simple, huh? The disk is wired to an electronic device which records exactly how far off-center (if at all) the jumper lands. The jumper with the lowest total score after a specified number of jumps wins the competition.

Style competition, like relative work, is not much of a spectator's event unless air-to-ground video is provided on a screen, as was the case at the 1988 Olympic opening ceremonies.

In style, the jumper exits the aircraft at 6,600

feet and performs a series of 360 degree turns and backloops that are watched and clocked from the ground, then reviewed by judges. Two flips, two left turns and two right turns complete the regimen. The jumper completing the regimen with the fastest time, including penalties, is the winner.

The very fact that Golden Knights are able to compete with other parachutists separates them from their counterpart aerial demonstration teams, the Thunderbirds and Blue Angels. The aerobatic skill of these jet teams is certainly breath-taking, but there's no means for them to prove their skill in competition except, of course, merely being chosen to pilot those teams puts them with the cream of the crop, just as the Knights are. The Knights, however, were formed with competition as part of their mission.

Prior to formation of the Army Parachute Team, international parachute competition was dominated by the French and by Eastern block countries. Although the sport of parachuting was growing in popularity in this country, it needed a "sponsor" of proportions which even the most discriminating Charlie Brown could appreciate. The Army was a logical choice.

Even before it was officially activated June 1, 1961 and called the U.S. Army Parachute Team, its members had taken fourth place overall at the 5th World Parachuting Championships held in Sofia, Bulgaria in 1960 and won America's first gold medal in a world competition. Since that year, the Golden Knights (the official nickname was adopted in 1962) have produced nearly a hundred national and two dozen individual world champions, and they've won more parachute titles than any other parachute team in the world, including Eastern-block parachute teams.

Treasures captured by the Knights in national and international competitions are brought home to the team's headquarters at Fort Bragg. The entire second floor of the team's dayroom holds about 60 percent of these gold, silver and bronze medals, as well as trophies, plaques, cups and other memorabilia earned during 30 years of competition.

Enclosed in glass cabinets lining the walls and a special, glass-encased area centered in the room, thousands of pieces of metal and strips of multicolored ribbon attest to victory, as do hundreds of silver-plated cups and plaques. And yet, every time the Knights leave Fort Bragg to participate in a parachute competition, the trophies and medals in this treasure room are squeezed together to make room for more.

Beams of golden sunlight slice through a door window at the opposite end of the room, causing the medals and trophies to sparkle, enhancing their aesthetic value for the men and women who have earned them over the years. But even if the gold medals were, in fact, gold and the silver medals and trophies were, in fact, silver, they'd be no more treasured by those who have served as Golden Knights and have left their mark on the history of this team with these spoils of their conquests.

As one stands at one end of the Knights' trophy room, surveying the glittering prizes before him, it's hard to imagine that this treasure chest represents little more than half of the medals and trophies won by the Golden Knights and not even a fraction of the titles, records and special honors bestowed upon the Golden Knights!

WHAT IS A GOLDEN KNIGHT?

The needle on each jumper's altimeter started moving as soon as the CH-47 helicopter lifted off Camp MacKall Airfield, well outside of Fort Bragg.

At 5,000 feet, the load-master lowered the tailgate/ramp. **Sergeant Jeff Steele**, part of the cadre for the Golden Knights' 1988 Tryout Committee, gave the loadmaster a ''thumb's up,'' stood and walked straight off the ramp, leaning forward as if trying to touch the sky.

Steele's early departure seemed to go un-noticed by the others. Their minds were oc-cupied with the perfor-mance expected of them. And yet, their in-dividual skills would help them less than their ability to work together as a team.

At 10,000 feet, four of the would-be Knights stood, checked their gear, then moved in a modified wedge forma-tion toward the ramp's edge. Three men and a woman wore intense

expressions as they grasped a lanyard leading down one leg to smoke canisters connected by a metal bracket to a glossy black French ''para'' boot.

At 12,000 feet, **Staff Sergeant Dave Haberkorn** joined his students on the ramp and, without speaking, turned and fell backward. His students followed close behind, pulling their lanyards, which released four trails of red smoke that marked their flight pattern for the ground cadre to observe. One day, they hoped, they would be observed by millions of cheering spectators.

Every year for nearly three decades, the Army Parachute Team has held ''tryouts'' to train and select new members. Golden Knights are selected for a 3-year tour, although some—particularly competitors, have remained longer.

To qualify to even apply for Golden Knights' tryouts, the applicant must be an active duty enlisted soldier with a minimum of 150 freefall jumps. He or she must also have a spotless military and civilian record, must meet Army height/weight standards and be eligible for reassignment if selected.

But what personality characteristics are expected of would-be Knights? And who is qualified to train and select such men and women who will someday represent both the U.S. Army and America? Perhaps some answers are found in questions asked us by children, for ''out of the mouths of babes'' come the most thought-provoking questions, directed with an innocent but sincere desire to learn.

Shortly after two members of the Army Parachute Team visited an elementary school near Fayetteville, North Carolina, a flurry of letters arrived at the team's headquarters.

One little lady, Amanda, colored a picture of herself at the bottom of her letter in which she

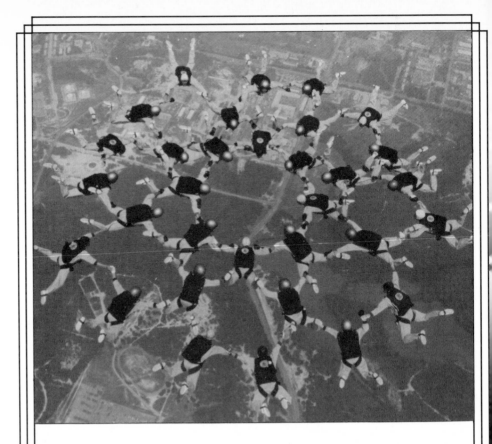

asked why Golden Knights jumped from airplanes at the "risc" (sic) of breaking a leg. She then added, "Do you get paid? Why?"

Amanda may have believed anyone simple-minded enough to jump from a perfectly good airplane didn't deserve financial compensation for taking such risks!

Jonathan was brief but a little more supportive. In fact, he offered the team his services. "If you need another 'parachuter'," he said, "just call me."

Although his spelling was a little weak, Thomas was the most perceptive student in his classroom.

"You are very good at that," he wrote. "How do you do it so 'purfick'? (sic) Whoever your coach is, he must be a good one."

Indeed, Thomas. Most people wowed by a Golden Knight aerial demonstration rarely take into consideration the training involved in such maneuvers. More importantly, few people inspired by the professional excellence displayed by Golden Knights consider the possibility that such qualities are inherent and common to each Knight, qualities that distinguish Golden Knights just as they do any top-level personnel in any field. They strive to be the best.

In order to give breath-taking, seemingly flawless performances, Golden Knights must train and train and train some more. Young Tom's question about the person responsible for such training deserves a response. Simply put, no single individual on the Army Parachute Team is conclusively more skilled than his or her peers to the extent that he or she can be "head coach."

The team is not only made up of, but it's run by NCO's who constantly critique each other to that unreachable point of perfection. To get started, however, the team must establish entry level standards through which new Knights come to the team.

The annual tryout program conducted each fall begins with applications from active duty soldiers from around the world. Each year, a changing number of applicants are selected for tryouts and invited to Fort Bragg for six weeks of rigorous training. Only the very best of these "wanna-be's" will be selected for positions on the team.

According to **Sergeant First Class Ben Currin**, the Gold Demonstration Team Leader, the tryout cadre aren't necessarily looking for the greatest parachutists in the world. "The team," he says, "doesn't expect a tryout to already demonstrate the parachuting skills of a Golden Knight, but the professional attitude demanded of a Golden Knight. It's easier," says Currin, "to train a good soldier to become a great parachutist than to take a great parachutist and try to make him or her into a good soldier.

"A professional demeanor and a willingness to sacrifice personal aspirations for the greater glory of the team is the gist of what it takes to be a Golden Knight," Currin says.

One former cadre member, Bob Finn, says the tryout cadre are not there to train anyone to become Golden Knights, but to find those who are already Golden Knights yet don't know it.

Still, all these attempts to define a Golden Knight fall short of the mark. It's much easier to describe a Golden Knight than to define a Golden Knight. And yet, such descriptions tend to build a definition.

The average Golden Knight is 26-years old. He or she represents the very best of their particular career management field (CMF). Each Knight maintains the highest level of efficiency in his military occupational specialty (MOS) while serving as a member of the team. Nearly every CMF is represented on the team, although combat arms MOS's—particularly Airborne-Infantry, Ranger and Special Forces—hold a strong majority.

The average Knight has served about five years in the Army, and the majority of those who have served on the team have made the Army a career. As such, Golden Knights represent many things—professional excellence, devotion to duty and a willingness to serve. Most of all, Golden Knights represent all the men and women of the U.S. Army and the nation they so proudly serve.

The key word is "represent," for that's what a Golden Knight does; that's what a Golden Knight is. The Golden Knights represent the United States Army and the finest precision freefall parachutists in the world. They are the Army's official ambassadors of goodwill. The following pages reveal the Golden Knights' colorful history and collective personality.

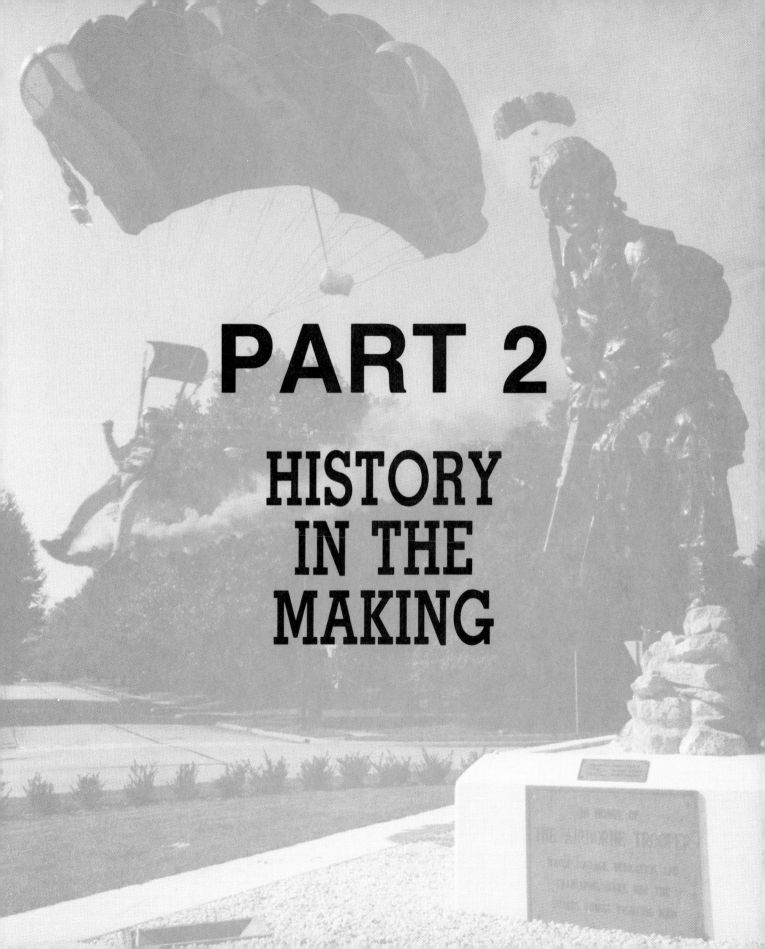

PART 2

HISTORY
IN THE
MAKING

PART 2

HISTORY IN THE MAKING

A SPORT IS BORN

Master SGT Ray Duffy posing with national championship medals.

There was no verbal declaration by our Maker which brought the U.S. Army Parachute Team suddenly into existence and placed it in the Airborne's Garden of Eden—Fort Bragg, North Carolina. In fact, the USAPT's formation wasn't sudden at all. Historical records even show two birthdates for the team—an unspecified day in September 1959 and an official activation date of June 1, 1961.

These two dates are not alone in the asserted history of the world's most famous parachute team. Some would argue the team owes its origins to the first American to compete in the World Parachuting Championships in 1954. **Sergeant Fred Mason**, U.S. Army, didn't win anything during this competition, but the undisputed fact that he competed as an American—an American soldier—makes his contribution worthy of inclusion in the history, if not prehistory, of the Golden Knights.

But if the exact date of the U.S. Army Parachute Team's conception is uncertain, one can trace the origin of the parachute itself. In 1495, universal genius Leonardo da Vinci drew a sketch of what he called a "tent roof." It depicted the stick figure of a man clinging to straps or harnesses connected to a two-dimensional, triangular-shaped object that could conceivably be used as a deceleration device. But deceleration from what?! There were no aircraft as yet (although da Vinci designed one of those, also) and ballooning wouldn't become popular for two more centuries. Needless to say, Leonardo could find no market for his parachute.

In 1617, another sketch of a parachute accompanied an article by yet another Italian (this one nameless to history, or at least to this writer). He, too, saw no market for a parachute and left it for French physicist Sebastien LeNormand to test the first parachute in 1783

by jumping from a water tower. Still, there was no demand for parachutes, probably because tower jumping never developed into a popular sport! Then in 1797, another Frenchman, Andre Jacques Garnerin, made a successful parachute jump from a balloon (one should note the word "successful" here in that, a few years before Garnerin, an unsuccessful attempt was made from a balloon—the jumper broke his leg on landing). From this time on, the parachute became a nice-to-have piece of equipment aboard balloons, which often times failed to stay in the air—usually at unhealthy altitudes!

The first parachutes were made of canvas, later silk, then nylon. Today's square canopy parachutes are made of a low porosity material called F-111. The round parachute canopy is given extraordinary strength by fabrication from up to 28 separate panels called "gores," each made of smaller sections sewn together in such a way that a tear is usually restricted to the section where it originates. Instead of gores, square canopies are designed with cells that catch the airflow, giving the parachute lift capability and a constant forward speed.

Improvements were made upon the parachute as new uses were found for it. With the advent of the airplane at the turn of the century, airplane pilots saw the parachute as an attractive alternative to landing a totally disabled airplane. The very first pilot to parachute from an airplane did so in 1912. He was **U.S. Army Captain Albert Berry**.

By the 1930's a genuine military aspect of the parachute was found in the form of the paratrooper, who was used extensively by both sides during World War II. The first airborne test platoon in this country was started in 1940 at Fort Bragg. In July 1990, American paratroopers —past and present, will celebrate their 50th anniversary in Washington, D.C.

Besides the military aspect of the parachute, American civilians also began to acquaint themselves with parachuting. American Jimmy Engels made the first stabilized "freefall" parachute jump in this country in 1936, and to prove it, he landed on the White House lawn. Engels was trained by French parachutists who, along with the Soviets, led the world in developing the growing sport of parachuting. That's right, sport. People were actually finding excuses to use their parachutes, leaving perfectly good airplanes, balloons or whatever jump platform available just for the thrill of falling through the air.

Another American, Joe Crane, was responsible for forming the first parachute club and training center in this country at Long Island in the late '30's. Crane called his club the "National Parachute Jumpers and Riggers Club." He is also credited with founding the Parachute Club of America, now called the U.S. Parachute Association. World War II and later, Korea, hampered the rush of jumping enthusiasts to join these clubs. Still, parachuting gradually grew in popularity, both as a sport for the participant and as a carnival act for spectators.

According to **Major** (retired) **Dick Bishop**, editor of *The DROP* magazine and associate of the early Army Parachute Team, the first sport parachute clubs in the Army were authorized in 1958 with the publishing of AR (Army Regulation) 95-19. The first of these clubs were the Special Warfare Center Sport Parachute Club (now called the Green Beret Club), the XVIII Airborne Corps Sport Parachute Club (now defunct) and the All American (82d Abn Div) Sport Parachute Club, all located at Fort Bragg. These clubs, in the words of **Captain** (retired) **Jim Perry**, first commander of the Army Parachute Team, were made up of "jockstrapping skydivers." As a former president of the Corps Club, Perry should know.

The parachute clubs gave paratroopers a chance to get in some extra jumps on weekends and to have fun with "tuck and tumble"—jumping without the restriction of that umbilical cord called a static line. According to Bishop, only a few members of these clubs could claim to be stable "delayed fall" jumpers, men like **Command Sergeant Major** (retired) **John Hollis**, who became the first first sergeant of the Army Parachute Team, and the aforementioned Jim Perry.

James "Jim" Perry was a U.S. Marine sergeant when he decided to accept a challenge in 1949 to parachute from one of the planes he had been learning to fly. Nine years later, he would resign his battlefield commission in the Marine Corps and accept a commission from the Army so he could "jump" and be a part of the Army's growing Special Forces. Upon his return from a behind-the-lines operation in Laos early in 1960, he was asked by Fort Bragg's Chief-of-Staff, Brigadier General Joseph W. Stilwell Jr., to take charge of the newly formed Strategic Army Corps (STRAC) Sport Parachute Team. Perry's leadership ultimately won this specially-formed team official recognition by the Department of the Army in 1961.

"John Hollis and I literally began the team with nothing and built it into what it is today," Perry said, while bestowing most of the credit on his first sergeant. "Both of us laugh together when it's asked, 'Jim Perry? Who in the world is Jim Perry?'"

Perry was actually third in line to serve as the officer-in-charge (OIC) of the STRAC Team, which had been formed at Fort Bragg in mid-September 1959 under the auspices of Brigadier General Stilwell. Many of the 13 members who comprised the STRAC Team were part of the all-Army national team that grabbed second place at the 2nd Adriatic Cup at Tivat, Yugoslavia in August 1959. Until that time, the Soviets had never been seriously challenged in a parachute competition. The Army team's successful first try at international competition proved the Soviets could be beaten.

"General Stilwell was so convinced that the Army needed a team of its own," Perry explained, "he sent me off as his emissary again and again, talking with anyone in the Pentagon who would listen and then help. There were some who saw merit in the competition schedule, but it was a period of austerity in the Army. No funds for frills. We had to prove ourselves in the demo field, show that (the team) enhanced recruiting in both the Army and the airborne."

Perry explained that

upon his return from Operation White Star in Laos in the spring of 1960, Perry, a young captain, was called into the office of the Chief-of-Staff, Brigadier General Stilwell. He was soon ordered by the general officer to take up a "French Cross" freefall position on the floor. With his face to the floor, arms rigidly at his side, back arched and his legs far apart and locked, anyone coming by the general's office at that moment might have wondered what this captain had done to be in such an embarrassing position.

When Perry had proven himself capable of performing the French Cross, Stilwell challenged the captain to teach him how it was done. Anyone now passing by the general's open door might have had heart failure to see Captain Perry standing over their chief of staff who lay face down on the floor, his legs and arms being positioned by the junior officer as if dealing with a prisoner of war.

Once satisfied that Perry knew enough about delayed fall jumping to teach it, Stilwell sent him to **Major Merrill Sheppard** as the Assistant OIC of the STRAC Team with the ultimate goal of making Perry the first commander of the U.S. Army Parachute Team. When Sheppard left the STRAC team a short time later to attend the "bootstrap" program, a special services officer was sent down from Corps, Perry says, "because someone thought we were just a bunch of jockstrapping skydivers." Perry says he lasted about two months. Stilwell then appointed him as the third OIC of the STRAC Team. In a year's time, Perry accomplished the mission he was given by Stilwell that day in the general's office.

Brigadier General Joseph W. Stilwell, Jr., son of General "Vinegar Joe" Stilwell, would ultimately become known as the father of the Army Parachute Team and military freefall. A 1933

graduate of the U.S. Military Academy, Stilwell served in the China-Burma-India Theater in World War II and as a commander of the 23rd Infantry Regiment in Korea. He attained the rank of brigadier general in 1956, the only star he'd ever receive.

According to Hollis, once Stilwell became a brigadier, he showed an extreme lack of fondness for colonels, saying it was not uncommon to see "a couple of full birds" standing at parade rest in front of Stilwell's desk. In 1959 he became the chief of staff of the XVIII Airborne Corps at Fort Bragg and began "rattling the cages" of every colonel on Fort Bragg to get support for the Army Parachute Team and other projects dear to him. He was still stepping on toes in the Special Warfare Center when he died in an airplane crash in 1966.

According to Perry, Stilwell squeezed funds from every athletic team at Fort Bragg to support the STRAC Team, which, not being a regular Army unit, had no funds or resources of its own. It was, in Perry's words, a Fort Bragg effort to start an "official" Army parachute team.

But because Stilwell had conceived of an official team from the beginning, it's easy to see why the team which eventually became an official Army unit would look back to 1959 as its beginnings. After all, Stilwell intended to make it an official team at its conception. Even so, as Perry would argue, there was a great deal of difference between the Fort Bragg team formed in 1959 and called STRAC and the one officially recognized by the Department of the Army in 1961 and activated as the United States Army Parachute Team.

"When you talk about the STRAC Sport Parachute Team," Perry conceded, "lay its credit to HALO (High Altitude, Low Opening) training on Sicily (Drop Zone) in 1958. Almost the entire Special Forces PS&M (Parachute Service & Maintenance) Rigger group took that initial training from **Jacques Istel**."

Istel and another Frenchman, **Lew Sanborn**, were naturalized Americans contracted by the U.S. Army to train seven American paratroopers in stabilized freefall techniques—men like **Specialist Four Dick Fortenberry, Sergeant Danny Byard** and **Lieutenant Roy Martin**, all of whom later became members of the STRAC Team and its prodigy—the Army Parachute Team.

"I was the first sergeant of the 77th Special Forces Rigger Detachment," said Hollis. "The HALO School started in my rigger shed in the old division area. Byard, Fortenberry...those guys first took the training from Jacques Istel, Lew Sanborn and their crew. I didn't make my first freefall parachute jump until St. Patrick's Day 1958."

According to Hollis, about the same time Istel and Sanborn trained Army paratroopers in delayed fall jumping (Nov-Dec 1957), the Army published AR 95-19, which helped "foster and encourage Army personnel to participate in parachute competitions and exhibition parachute activities." The seven soldiers trained by Istel and Sanborn then trained eight more paratroopers in freefall techniques (Feb-Apr 1958). Of these 15, most went back to their units and formed clubs to train other paratroopers in delayed fall jumping. A few of them started the Special Forces HALO School, a story being published at this time by Dick Bishop, who became part of the HALO Program in the early '60's.

"Brigadier General Stilwell wanted a team to put on demonstrations," Hollis said. "So, he picked Major Sheppard, who picked me and we got all the people from my rigger detachment and a couple others on post (Fort Bragg), as well as three or four from Fort Campbell and one or two from Fort Benning. That's how the STRAC Team got started."

Newly formed, the 12 enlisted paratroopers and one jumping officer immediately began training for a combination demonstration-competition schedule. Their very first demonstration was in Danville, Virginia, November 1, 1959. By year's end, the STRAC Team had performed seven parachute demonstrations. During the 1960 demonstration season, the new team completed the world's first five-way baton pass from 30,000 feet above El Centro, California. For all its successes, however, the name "STRAC Team" wasn't exactly drawing crowds. Acronyms, though loved by the Army, aren't so well received by the American public.

"STRAC?" People would always ask, "What's STRAC?"

A news release written by the team's PIO (Public Information Officer), **Sergeant Don Kidd**, May 2, 1960, noted the STRAC Team had decided to change its name to the U.S. Army "Sport" Parachute Team, a new name, but still no official recognition by the Department of the Army. Everyone on the team was attached there from other units. When the team obtained its official recognition 13 months later, it dropped "sport" from its already adopted name.

"Captain Perry and General Stilwell started working together to form (officially) the Army Parachute Team," Hollis said. "They had to go through the Continental Army Command at Fort Monroe, Virginia. Captain Perry spent most of the time running back and forth up there. There were no other officers at that time, so I was having to coordinate everything."

Perry's efforts proved successful, he says, only because Hollis was able to keep the team running without him. Hollis' NCO leadership set a precedent existing to this day as it remains a team made up of, and run by Non-Commissioned Officers (NCOs). NCOs not only conduct but plan the training. NCOs select the show schedule, and they coordinate and lead parachute demonstrations and competitions with only minimal guidance by their commander, executive officer and operations officer.

The Army's "NCO team" performed for more than 11 million spectators in 25 different states in 1960. In addition to picking up more and more demonstrations that year, the team was entering and winning parachute competitions. At the 5th World Championships held in Bulgaria, the fledgling Army team represented the United States, earning a gold and a silver medal.

At age 20, **Specialist Four Jim Arrender**'s gold medal in Style made him not only the youngest, but very first American to win a gold medal in a world parachute competition. **Specialist Five Richard**

"Dick" Fortenberry, who took fourth place in Accuracy, made the first ever dead-center landing and scored enough points to win the silver medal as second place overall. Thanks to the Army team, the United States finished fourth place in its first serious attempt to compete in a world parachute championship—a tremendous accomplishment in a sport that, until now, Americans had been considerably lacking.

Between January and May 1961, the team underwent personnel changes, adding and deleting to obtain both the best jumpers and best soldiers, as well as those with some longevity in their enlistments. They also "played politics," according to John Hollis. That is, in order to secure the official blessings of the Department of the Army, the team performed at Fort Monroe, Virginia for the Continental Army Command, met several U.S. senators and toured the country with the specific purpose of

showing off the Army to those people able to do something for the team.

On May 18, 1961, an order was issued which activated the U.S. Army Parachute Team, effective June 1st as a special unit with 15 enlisted and four officers. Its mission was threefold: first, to serve as a recruiting tool for the Army and the airborne through aerial demonstrations

and public performances, enhancing the Army's image; second, compete in national and international parachute competitions; third, provide a base of highly skilled parachutists who research and develop parachuting techniques and equipment.

During the early years of the Army Parachute Team, the Army tasked the team to document its

---

EARNING A NAME

After 21 months of "tryouts," Joe Stilwell finally realized his dream of an official Army team. The morning report of June 1, 1961 listed the following soldiers present for duty at the newly activated unit called the U.S. Army Parachute Team:

CPT JAMES PERRY . . . . COMMANDER
MSG JOHN HOLLIS . . . . FIRST SERGEANT
1LT ROY MARTIN . . . . EXECUTIVE OFFICER
2LT JAMES PEARSON . . . . OPERATIONS OFFICER
2LT DOUGLAS RUNNELS . . PUBLIC AFFAIRS OFFICER
SFC GERALD BOURQUIN . . . . PARACHUTIST
SGT LOY BRYDON . . . . PARACHUTIST
SGT DANNY BYARD . . . . PARACHUTIST
SGT WILFRED CHARETTE . . . . PARACHUTIST
SFC WILLIAM EDGE . . . . PARACHUTIST
SP5 RICHARD FORTENBERRY . . . . PARACHUTIST
PFC KEITH JORGENSEN . . . . PARACHUTIST
SP4 BOBBY LETBETTER . . . . PARACHUTIST
SFC HERALD LEWIS . . . . PARACHUTIST
SP4 COY McDONALD . . . . PARACHUTIST
PFC ROBERT McDONNELL . . . . PARACHUTIST
SGT JOE NORMAN . . . . PARACHUTIST
SFC RALPH PALMER . . . . PARACHUTIST
PFC ROY SMITH . . . . PARACHUTIST

historic freefall training. Most of that documentation was taped in freefall by team members who wore heavy cameras attached to the side of their helmets. Much of that footage was released to the man who got the Army started in freefall parachuting—Jacques Istel. According to Perry, Istel used that footage to produce a short documentary on the sport of freefall parachuting called "A Sport is Born." Although rough footage by today's standards, it showed the non-jumping public the world as seen through the eyes of parachutists sailing towards earth.

The documentary made a name for Istel and the sport of parachuting and was a pleasant introduction of the Army team to the world. And though the sport had been around for more than two decades now, through the birth of the Army Parachute Team, it was certainly re-born. During the years to follow, all parachute teams would

model themselves after the team calling itself the "USAPT," later to be known to the world as **the Golden Knights.**

Later that summer, **Pvt. James Overmyer** was attached to the team as its company clerk, along with **Sgt. Bob Turner**—an Army photographer. The men who made up this historic unit knew the easy part of their mission was over—getting official recognition. According to Jim Perry, "now we had to prove ourselves" to be worth the Army's money.

And very little money at that. Perry estimates their first year's budget was only $55,000. This money, he says, was meant to pay for per diem for each man while traveling, the cost of traveling itself, as well as the parachute and supporting equipment the team used in parachute demonstrations and competitions. It was, however, a considerable improvement over the zero-dollars budget authorized the former STRAC Team.

According to John

The Cleveland Air Show, September 1989.

Coy O. MacDonald, first place winner 1963 Adriatic Cup in Yugoslavia, member of 1964 men's national team. He also holds more accuracy records than any man in the world—58 records total.

Hollis, much of the office furniture and equipment the team had was "acquired" from another unit at Fort Bragg, probably the 82d Airborne Division. It was neither borrowed nor stolen, he explained:

"We were training out at one of the drop zones one day and one of the guys discovered a cache of excess equipment," he said, chuckling. "The stuff was just piled there, half-camouflaged. Some unit was obviously trying to hide it during an IG (Inspector General) Inspection. We just did them a favor and hid it back at the team area."

According to Don Kidd, much of the surplus equipment would later be replaced following a walk-through inspection at the team area by Joe Stilwell. When Stilwell saw his team was operating with run-down furniture, one typewriter with several non-working keys and second-hand sewing machines used to make repairs to surplus (surplus!) parachute canopies, he exploded. Within a few hours of Stilwell's visit, Kidd said a pair of two-and-a-half-ton trucks pulled up in front of the team headquarters and began unloading uncrated, brand-new parachutes, sewing machines, desks and, for the PIO—Don Kidd, a new typewriter.

"He (Stilwell) transferred $15,000 for us to buy the first black and gold Pioneer TU's we used to take us to a victory at Orange (Massachusetts) in 1962," Perry said. "The Russians even wanted to buy one from us when the meet was over."

Before that time, the team had been using the old Conquistadors, which today is part of the unit patch designed by the Institute of Heraldry in 1969. The Conquistador was actually a standard round canopy used by the Army with some notable changes made by the Army Parachute Team. Huge holes were cut in the panels, allowing more maneuverability.

Pioneer worked out a special deal allowing the team a discount rate on newer model parachutes (upon which the Army team would also make changes) in exchange for the Pioneer company being able to advertise their outfitting the Army Parachute Team.

"We lent them our name and fame, and they gave us a break on parachute equipment," Perry said. "They devised a Para-Sail which could be towed in the air, and we modified it into the Para-Commander."

Not having enough money was a constant problem, sometimes even threatening to shut it down. In those early days, the lack of per diem (money used by soldiers on temporary duty for food and lodging) was a thorn in the flesh that even Stilwell couldn't dislodge.

"We ran out of per diem money very soon in the first year, even though it was parceled out in $5 bills just as pocket money for two or three-day demos,"

Perry explained. "We were always at the mercy of a show sponsor for food and lodging. Our meals consisted of no more than a few hot-dogs. During one demo in Virginia, we even had to sleep under some bleachers."

Despite a shortage of funds, the team stayed on the road for demonstrations and competitions 267 days in 1961. The "Cutaway" maneuver was first implemented into the show that same year, and even today, will draw a collective gasp from the crowd. While competing in France, the army chutists took the gold medal in all individual events and won top team honors as well—the first of many victories over the Soviets.

Hollis said in those days everyone on the team was also a jumper. During one show in New York, the team divided itself into two groups, allowing each group to jump at a different location.

"Four of us jumped at Suffolk County after getting a ride up there on a Husky (helicopter)," Hollis laughed. "It was Jim Perry, myself, Roy Martin and our team photographer—Bob Turner who'd never jumped a demonstration in his life. But we put him out the door anyway and he did all right. It was real windy, too. We all hit like sacks of rocks, especially Turner. Then we caught a National Guard helicopter back to New York."

Because the team lacked an organic aviation section in those days, Hollis said they seldom knew what type of jump platform they'd be using until the morning of the show. During a show in nearby Wilmington, North Carolina, September 24, 1961, the team suffered its first tragedy when the C-123 cargo plane in which the team was riding crashed during takeoff. Hollis received a broken back in that crash. **Bob McDonnell** was badly burned over most of his body. Three other team members—**Joe Norman, Bobby Letbetter** and **Wilfred Charette**, were also injured. The team's photographer, **Bob Turner**, was killed.

"After the crash, our enemies wanted to kill the team," Perry said. "I had to say again and again, 'The Army Parachute Team didn't crash at Wilmington. Our jump platform crashed.' We were just unfortunate passengers in the plane. Still, they wanted to finish us off after the crash. But Joe Stilwell—God bless him—acted as our Guardian Angel."

Most of the team's "enemies" were field commanders who simply didn't think the Army's image was best represented by "jock-strapping skydivers" touring the country, Perry explained. He and Stilwell had several harsh battles with the team's opponents after the crash—the result of which, Perry believes, ultimately saved the team, but may have caused him to sacrifice his career.

Perry and **Sergeant First Class Herald "Harry" Lewis**, demonstration team leader, were in Venezuela training the Venezuelan Falcons (parachute team) when the crash occurred. Upon his immediate return, Perry, through Stilwell, ensured burn victim McDonnell and the team's public affairs officer—**Lieutenant Doug Runnels**, were awarded the Soldier's Medal for their heroic actions during the crash. The Soldier's Medal is one of the highest peacetime awards given by the Army for heroic action involving the risk of one's own life to save another's.

Despite the harassing efforts to dismantle the Army Parachute Team after the Wilmington crash, Perry said the team sold itself and continued to grow in fame. And the more famous the team became, the harder it became to shut it down.

"We didn't have one bummer in the group," Perry said. "Everyone was gregarious, willing to work hard and to make personal sacrifices. Every official we met thought we were the epitome of the United States Army soldier. Recruitment for the airborne was up because of our demos, and so they gave us extra men."

Perry said the new men were to be temporaries, meant to help the team meet the increasing number of demonstrations. Most of those temporaries were authorized after the crash, he said. Among those brought to the team at that time were **Staff Sergeant Ray Duffy** and **Sergeant First Class Gene Thacker**, both of whom became national champions on the team. The Army would authorize the team's strength to grow to 42 enlisted and seven officers in 1963, which allowed them to keep these temporaries and others, thus being able to divide itself into two demonstration teams and a competition team, plus a support element.

By 1962 the team was in great demand for demonstrations, and it had proven to be fully capable of besting the Soviets in competition—

a genuine plus in those Cold War days. Still, there had to be something else the USAPT could do to increase its fame. Perry said they thumbed through the record books and found that no one had ever touched on the 1,000 meter clear-and-pull accuracy records, either individual or team, so he asked the Army for aviation support and permission to go to Yuma, Arizona. Four weeks later, in February 1962, the United States was listed in the record books, thanks to the Army Parachute Team, who broke all 19 existing 1,000 meter accuracy jumps. The following year, the USAPT broke an additional 48 records, and for the first time, the Soviets were in second place in the record books, which for the most part had been authored by them.

Mimicking an unidentified official in the Pentagon, Perry said, excitedly, '''We got ourselves some kind of propaganda machine down there!'''

The Army's demonstration team was proving to be even more useful to the Defense Department in some ways than the Air Force Thunderbirds or the Navy Blue Angels. Before the USAPT, the Army had, in Hollis' words, a helicopter "square dance" team that really didn't do a lot for recruitment, except perhaps in aviation. The USAPT, however, not only performed, but had won special recognition for the U.S. in world-class competitions, and had now put the Americans in the record books.

Reinforcing their growing image, the team took second place overall at the 6th World Championships in Orange, Massachusetts in 1962. Jim Arrender, now a civilian, became the overall world champion, while Dick Fortenberry took third place overall. The team received a morale boost, says Perry, when Bob McDonnell, who had been hospitalized for nearly a year since the crash, came to

Orange to cheer his teammates on to victory.

According to Ray Duffy, McDonnell was determined to make a jump while he was there at Orange despite having lost most of his left hand in the plane fire. His teammates rigged his parachute specially for him so he could steer it, once under canopy. They joined McDonnell in his personal "victory" jump, which was symbolic of the "overcoming spirit" of the group.

"I could never have survived that crash or all that time in the hospital were it not for the support of my teammates," McDonnell told dinner guests at the Knights' 20th Reunion, December 9, 1989. "I'm here today because of them."

McDonnell, who now teaches high school English, still wears the scars of that crash, despite more than two dozen surgical operations. And yet, he takes great pride in having served as a member of the Army Parachute Team, and to this day, he's still jumping out of airplanes and he's an active competition judge.

After their second successful world championships, the members of the USAPT, minus Perry, got together to come up with an official nickname, similar to the Air Force and Navy teams. On October 15, 1962, the votes were counted and the USAPT would become known as the GOLDEN KNIGHTS. "Knights"...champions of principle and conquest, alluding to the fact that the USAPT had "conquered the skies." "Golden"...signifying that the team had the reputation of bringing home gold medals and its chosen colors were black and gold—taken from the U.S. Military Academy at West Point, New York.

West Point was noted for producing some of the finest officers in the Army and, by now, the USAPT was acknowledged as some of the finest enlisted soldiers in the Army. Black and gold were also the colors of other super-elite units like the Rangers and the 101st Airborne Division. When the decision was finalized among team members, they brought the idea of "The Golden Knights" before their commander, Jim Perry.

"The golden who?!" Perry chided them humorously. "What's that suppose to be, some kind of blues band? No way. We earned our name as the U.S. Army Parachute Team, and that's the name we'll keep as long as I'm commander of this team."

Perry said he refused to let the team stencil "GOLDEN KNIGHTS" on any equipment or office stationery—team, personal or otherwise. He even forbade team members from referring to themselves as "Golden Knights" to the press. He was convinced a nickname would rob the team of the fame it had earned as the U.S. Army Parachute Team. After all, the team had already undergone two name changes, beginning as the STRAC Team, then the U.S. Army Sport Parachute Team. They had dropped "sport" off the name to disassociate themselves from all the other sport parachute "clubs." The USAPT was not a club, Perry emphasized, but an official Army unit with a military mission.

That same month, however, Perry was offered the position of Airborne Advisor to the Venezuelan Parachute Battalion and he took it. Laughing about it today, he says that "within five minutes after I signed out of Fort Bragg, they had GOLDEN KNIGHTS stamped on every piece of equipment, every building and every rock in the team area!"

Despite Perry's fears, however, the official nickname didn't require the team to start its reputation anew. The new nickname was shorter and easier for the public to accept and remember than the rather lengthy title of United States Army Parachute Team. In 1969, the team celebrated its thousandth aerial demonstration and 10 years of performing and competing for the Army in a demonstration in Yuma, Arizona, where the team now had a propensity to be drawn each year for winter training.

By the end of their first decade, the average Knight was a more experienced jumper than his predecessors on the STRAC Team. Each jumper averaged 850 jumps now, which was roughly twice the average number of jumps of STRAC Team members. Today that average is closer to 1000. Also the average Knight presently is more than three years younger than the average STRAC Team member. Another even more notable difference of today's team is found in the members themselves. The original 13 members of the STRAC Team were all men. Since 1977, the Army Parachute Team has consisted of men and women, both representing the very

best in the sport of parachuting and some of the finest soldiers in the Army.

In 1974, the U.S. Parachute Association, formerly the Parachute Club of America, recognized the Golden Knights with its highest honor—the USPA Achievement Award, for their many achievements in the sport called ''skydiving'' by civilians but ''precision freefall parachuting'' by the Golden Knights. What is the difference?

Any Knight would gladly explain that the major difference between ''skydiving'' and ''precision freefall parachuting'' is: the former is for pleasure, and the latter is for work and pleasure! The Golden Knights are professionals in a sport that's both dangerous and enjoyable. They are tasked by the Army to research military aspects of the sport, while demonstrating the precision which can be obtained through continuous training.

Skydiving, Perry ex-

plained, conjures up an image of someone diving from an aircraft with the utmost ease, just as one might do from a springboard. The team took great lengths to distance itself from the days when parachuting was a carnival act—an act that Perry himself had made extra money doing in the late '40's. Each Golden Knight maneuver—maneuver, NOT stunt, Perry emphasized—is carefully orchestrated and practiced by team members with safety as the overriding factor above entertainment. And anyone who's ever experienced—experienced, not just observed—a Golden Knight aerial demonstration can testify to its entertainment value.

Because of their commitment to safety, the Golden Knights have made nearly 10 million parachute jumps since their patriarchs first began training, performing and competing in 1959. And yet, in 30 years of freefall parachuting, the Army Parachute Team has

Candles are lighted during memorial services for 14 deceased members of the U.S.A.P.T., The Golden Knights, by SFC Francis M. Brownfield, left, and PFC Jack Brake at the Ft. Bragg Main Post Chapel on 13 Mar 1973.

suffered only seven parachute-related fatalities. Their reputation for a spectacular but safe performance is yet another reason the team stays in high demand on the air show circuit. As a TV news anchor once commented, "The Golden Knights have truly earned their golden reputation."

WINNING A NATION

At a demonstration on Coney Island, New York in 1961, the Army Parachute Team thrilled 1.25 million spectators in a single show. It wasn't to be the team's largest audience, but an indication of what was to come during the years ahead. From the seven demos performed by the STRAC Team in 1959 to the 348 performed by the Golden Knights in 1989, aerial enthusiasts in all 50 states and 42 foreign countries have had the opportunity to watch and, more importantly, meet the U.S. Army's official ambassadors.

But as John Hollis explained, when the team first began performing aerial demonstrations, there really were no precedents to follow except the old carnival acts. Those acts consisted of little more than exiting the aircraft and landing close enough to the crowd for them to see the jumper was a real person and not a "wind dummy." To attract larger crowds, these jumpers often took unnecessary risks— called "stunts" by the media.

The axiom, "Golden Knights don't do 'stunts'," is taught to every team tryout upon his or her arrival. The maneuvers the team has incorporated into its shows were developed after careful consideration of all the risks involved and the subsequent elimination of those risks through American ingenunity which enabled them to modify their equipment to meet new demands for it and through thousands upon thousands of practice jumps.

The "cutaway" maneuver was introduced into the team's show late in 1961 by the Research & Development segment of the team. It remains a breathless demonstration to spectators who unconsciously count seconds as minutes, as one chute appears to fail and is released. Several more "minutes" appear to elapse before the jumper, now in freefall, deploys another chute.

The "max track" maneuver was entered in the free-lance competition at the Adriatic Cup in 1963 and won. It had already been a regular part of the Golden Knights' air show for two years. The "max track" consisted of two jumpers exiting the plane at the same time and "tracking" 180 degrees away from each other. These jumpers sometimes landed more than five miles apart. Ray Duffy said they eventually modified the "max track" to the "diamond track" performed today simply because they never

knew where their jumpers were going to land, which always made it difficult to link them back up with the rest of the team. More importantly, neither of these jumpers were able to be there for the team line up or to "work the crowd."

"Working the crowd" is the part of the Golden Knights' performance that really separates their demonstration team from all others. Unlike jet demonstration teams, which are impressive in flight, the pilots of these shiney machines remain a mystery to the crowds. Golden Knights, however, do their remarkable feats of aerobatics, then land among the spectators in order to autograph team posters and brochures, answer questions about the sport of parachuting and the Army, or quite simply, to win the approval of the American people. The team does this by one-on-one contact with children and adults at air shows, during hospital visits and through presentations at

Bobby "Spider" Wrenn, Golden Knight from 1966-1969 and 1977-1981, lands with his spider silhouetted on his parachute canopy that gave him his nickname. However, he earned the name years earlier while attending Fayetteville High School.

high schools and universities. In one year—1978, for example, the team made 778 public appearances, only 235 of which were actual parachute demonstrations.

Rarely does the team cancel a show and only then after the safety factors were overriding.

Mere inconvenience is not a factor. If spectators are willing to gather in harsh weather, the Knights will perform for their fans. During a show in Vermont in 1963, the team jumped in four-feet of snow, a jump that would not be soon forgotten by the spectators or the

jumpers! In 1989, the team jumped onto a wooden raft measuring no more than 40-feet by 80-feet and anchored along the intercoastal waterway in Ocean City, Maryland. Winds were high and the water—as water tends to be—was wet! Few people among the crowds who watched these demos understood the timing and precision involved in doing a jump under these conditions, yet everyone understood that the parachutists they saw were true professionals. The Knights did the jump and, as always, hit the target.

Over the years, the Knights have performed in all 50 states, showing off for the 49th state, Alaska, in 1967; then Hawaii in 1970. During an average show season, the team will perform in more than two-thirds of the states in hundreds of cities across the country. Each show season begins in early March and ends by late November. During those months, Golden Knights travel all over the nation, performing the same level of perfection, show after show, crowd after crowd, with never-ending enthusiasm for the job they do.

In essence, the U.S. Army Parachute Team is an American show force without weapons or armor. These Knights without armor are often called upon to show the American flag in places or during ceremonies where they become good-will ambassadors for our nation. In February 1984, barely 90 days after the rescue of American students on the island nation of Grenada, the Golden Knights did an aerial demonstration for the people of Grenada and the news media. Staff Sergeant Jeanne Lasher became the first woman to jump into the island nation. Another lady, however, Sergeant Annie Gallagher, who would try out for and make the team later that year, was already a Grenada veteran. She was part of the 319th Military Intelligence Battalion who supported the combat troops that cleared the island of Cuban resistance.

Four years before the Grenada demo, the Knights were invited to jump with the American and Olympic flags in Lake Placid, New York, for the opening ceremonies of the 1980 Winter Olympics. In 1988, the Knights were part of another Olympic ceremony, this time the Summer Olympics in Seoul, South Korea. Americans watching via satellite saw the five Olympic rings (three rings over two) being formed in freefall above the Olympic stadium. The gold ring, appropriately enough, was made up entirely of Golden Knights.

Only a few days after the 1988 presidential elections, the inauguration committee contacted the Knights' operations office. Two months later, in a quiet ceremony before a few million friends, relatives and spectators (live and via satellite), the Golden Knights performed for their new commander-in-chief, President-elect George Bush. They landed on the lawn behind the Lincoln Memorial in Washington, D.C. under the close scrutiny of Secret Service agents, who probably didn't know Jimmy Engels started the sport in this country in 1936 with a similar aerial demonstration.

While these particular demonstrations are note-

Many noteworthy performances of the Golden Knights have helped the team win the esteem of their countrymen, and the benevolence of many of our allies, including the following:

NIAGARA FALLS	NIAGARA FALLS, NEW YORK
THE STATUE OF LIBERTY	NEW YORK CITY
THE WORLD TRADE CENTER	NEW YORK CITY
MOUNT RUSHMORE	KEYSTONE, NORTH DAKOTA
THE GOLDEN GATE BRIDGE	SAN FRANCISCO, CALIFORNIA
STONE MOUNTAIN	STONE MOUNTAIN, GEORGIA
WRIGHT BROTHERS' NATIONAL MEMORIAL	KITTYHAWK, N.C.
THE GATEWAY ARCH	ST. LOUIS, MISSOURI
DIAMOND HEAD STATE MONUMENT	HONOLULU, HAWAII
CONEY ISLAND AMUSEMENT PARK	BROOKLYN, NEW YORK
WORLD'S FAIR	KNOXVILLE, TENNESSEE
XVIII WINTER OLYMPICS	LAKE PLACID, NEW YORK
NFL PRO BOWL	HONOLULU, HAWAII
NFL SUPER BOWL	PASADENA, CALIFORNIA
MAJOR LEAGUE BASEBALL WORLD SERIES	NEW YORK CITY
ANGEL OF PEACE MEMORIAL	WEST BERLIN, WEST GERMANY
INTERNATIONAL AIR SALON	PARIS, FRANCE
1986 AMERICA'S CUP TRIALS	FERMANTILE, AUSTRALIA
THE OPERA HOUSE	SIDNEY, AUSTRALIA
ABBOTSVILLE INTERNATIONAL AIR SHOW	ABBOTSVILLE, CANADA
QUEEN'S PARK	ST. GEORGE'S ISLAND, GRENADA
GATOR BOWL	GAINSVILLE, FLORIDA
1988 SUMMER OLYMPICS	SEOUL, SOUTH KOREA
FIESTA BOWL	PHOENIX, ARIZONA
PRESIDENTIAL INAUGURATION	WASHINGTON, D.C.
COTTON BOWL	DALLAS, TEXAS

worthy events and places, every demo is important to the Golden Knights. Every town, every performance is regarded as special. That's why team members are always so well-received by the American people, whose respect the Knights have won through hundreds of thousands of aerial demonstrations and public performances.

WINNING THE WORLD

Over 725 trophies, an equal number of medals and nearly 2,000 cups, plaques, plates and other trinkets testifying to victory line the walls of the Golden Knights' trophy room. And yet, the booty contained within those walls represent little more than half the team's winnings through 30 years of parachute competition. In a sport that Americans had been totally shut out of until the late 1950's, the name "Golden Knights" would ultimately bring fear, sometimes anger, but always respect into the hearts of parachute competitors around the world.

Part of the team's mission statement when it was formally activated in 1961 stated that the team was formed to compete in national and international parachute competitions. It was hoped the team might win some recognition for the United States, particularly in international competition. No one ever dreamed the Golden Knights would exceed their mission statement above and beyond the call of duty. Since 1959, the Army Team has never lost face in the national championships. In fact, the team so dominates the sport in this country, it has never failed to place at least one team member on the U.S. Parachute Team to compete in the World Championships.

Ray Duffy believes the sport itself flourishes to-day partly because of the Golden Knights, noting that former members of the team continue in the sport after they leave the team and the Army. Ray pointed out that the 1960 World Style Champion, Jim Arrender, was a civilian when he became the overall world champion in 1962. Likewise, former three-time national champion, Sergeant Clay Schoepple, was a civilian when he became overall world champion in 1972. Former commanders of the team like Roy Martin and Chris Needels have served on the Board of Directors of the United States Parachute Association. Numerous Golden Knights have served as chief judges and event judges at national and international competitions, such as Phil Miller, Gene Thacker, Ace Bunkhard and, yes, even Ray Duffy.

It was at the 2nd Adriatic Cup in 1958 at Tivat, Yugoslavia that the Americans first made a significant showing in an interna-tional parachute competition. The next Adriatic Cup was postponed due to the "Coup de Monde" in 1961, held at Laferte-Gaucher, France. When finally held, the Americans, now official-ly represented by the U.S. Army, took everything. For the first time the U.S. Parachute Team defeated the Soviets and the French who had been sharing domination of interna-tional parachute com-petition. Later, at the 3rd Adriatic Cup in 1963 at Portoroz, Yugoslavia, the U.S. Army team captured first and se-cond place individual honors through the ef-forts of staff sergeants Coy O. McDonald and Joe Norman.

At the world cham-pionships, Jim Arrender and Dick Fortenberry were becoming the forces to beat as the Army team gathered momentum. Arrender, who grabbed the gold medal in Style in 1960, took overall honors in 1962. Fortenberry, who took second place overall in 1960, dropped

prus Gardens.

down to third in 1962, but returned with a vengeance in 1964 to take overall honors. During that same year at the U.S. Nationals, Fortenberry earned the overall title for a third straight year. He then became specially honored by having that trophy retired to him and the Golden Knights.

Throughout the sixties and seventies, the Golden Knights continued to dominate every major parachute competition in which they competed. With the entrance of the first woman on the team in 1977, Cheryl Stearns, the Golden Knights added a new dimension to its competitive achievements. Stearns, who had already proven herself a lethal opponent in women's events, has dominated women's style & accuracy from 1974 through the present. By 1984, she began to get some serious competition from within her own ranks. Terry Bennett Vares, formerly one of the Knights' demonstrators, put away her smoke

63

brackets in 1982 to try her skill at competition. During the world meet in 1986, she became the second female Golden Knight to earn a world title. Now the team could justifiably say they had produced the very best parachutists in the world, male and female.

With the inclusion of relative work in parachute competition in the '70's, the Golden Knights responded by fielding a team from members of its demo teams, who took first place at the Southeastern Parachute Conference Meet in 1972. Three years later, relative work was officially entered as a parachuting event for the world championships, thus dividing world parachuting competition. Style & Accuracy would continue to be held on even-numbered years, and Relative Work would be held on odd-numbered years. In 1981, at the 4th World Parachuting Championships of Relative Work held in Zephyrhills, Florida, the Knights took their first world championship in relative work by winning the 4-way event.

According to one of the '81 champions—Andy Gerber, the team then began concentrating on the 8-way event and rebuilding itself after several team members received overseas assignments. In 1987 and again in 1989, the Knights won the 8-way event at the world meet. In '87 they also took the silver medal in the 4-way event and, although they were the '89 National champions in 4-way, the team declined to compete in that event at the world meet, deciding to concentrate on the 8-way event where competition from the Soviets and French was intensifying.

No matter how many medals are brought home by the Golden Knights from parachute competitions, there's yet another benefit the sport lends to the team and

The following members of the U.S. Army Parachute Team have earned a gold medal at a World Parachute Championship:

JIM ARRENDER '60,'62	TERRY BENNETT VARES '84,'86
DICK FORTENBERRY '64	CHRIS WAGNER '87,'89
JACK BRAKE '76	SCOTT RHODES '87,'89
CHUCK COLLINGWOOD '76	PAUL RAFFERTY '87,'89
CHERYL STEARNS '78,'82,'86	WILLIE LEE '87,'89
ANDY GERBER '81,'87,'89	JIM COFFMAN '87,'89
GLENN BANGS '81	MATT DAVENPORT '87
BOB FINN '81	CHAS HEEGEMAN '87
MARK GABRIEL '81	CRAIG GIRARD '89
MIKE DEVEAULT '81	KEVIN PEYTON '89
MAURICE FERNANDEZ '82	TODD LORENZO '89

*Former Golden Knight Clay Schoepple won overall champion in 1972, less than one year after leaving the team and the Army. He was the first American to win an overall title since Dick Fortenberry won that title in 1964.

the nation. As then Sergeant First Class Phil Miller explained in a radio interview in 1964, sports have a way of transcending political boundaries.

"The common bond of interests which exist between parachutists on an international scale is difficult to describe," Miller said. "You have to experience it to fully appreciate it."

As a planner for the 7th World Championships, Miller set up a rest and relaxation cruise for all 32 nations competing. It gave competitors a chance to meet and associate with each other on neutral grounds and a chance to share their common bond—the sport of parachuting.

Little more than a year later, the Knights interacted with an allied parachute team—the British Red Devils, who came to Fort Bragg to train with the Knights. According to Duffy, the Red Devils challenged them to a game of soccer in which the Knights were thoroughly beaten to a pulp! After losing to the British at their own game, the Americans, in turn, challenged them to a game of basketball. This time it was the British who were beaten to a pulp! The friendships made through these humbling defeats were everlasting. Had their opponents been Soviets, Duffy believes the outcome would have been the same—peace could be found though sports competition, as men and women relate to each other not as nationalists, but as human beings with the same skills and emotions.

Since the Army Parachute Team was formed as a base of highly skilled parachutists, they have lent their expertise to allied nations, training their soldiers in freefall techniques. Each November, for example, the German Army Parachute Team comes to Fort Bragg for several weeks to train with the Golden Knights. In November 1989, 11 Golden Knights traveled to Australia to train with them and compete in the Royal Australian Army Military Nationals. The Knights made a fairly clean sweep of nearly every event, which included individual and team Style & Accuracy, 4-way Relative Work and Canopy Relative Work. They also conducted several workshop seminars on relative work and on Style & Accuracy, to help the Aussies progress in the sport. And yet, assistance is not limited to allies in the field of competition.

During the 1988 World Cup competition in Vichy, France, members of the Knights' relative work team gave pointers to their Soviet opponents, who were unfamiliar with one of the aircraft being used as a jump platform. The exchange of dialogue between the two teams was genuine and sincere. The two most powerful nations in the world were no longer fighting the "Cold War" through parachute competitions. They were simply competing as friendly rivals in a sport enjoyed by citizens of

The 1961 crash at Wilmington, North Carolina. Members of the Army Parachute Team were aboard the Thunderbird's cargo plane, a C-123, when it went down on takeoff. One team member was killed, several severely injured.

both countries. Even if the Knights had not won that competition (which they did) they won something greater—the respect of a worthy opponent.

SURVIVING DISASTER

The view from the port-hole-sized windows was limited to only a few feet, due to fog, as the F27 Fokker descended in preparation to land at Simmons Army Airfield. It was early January 1989. Weather conditions were about as expected for that time of year and the team's pilots—Captain James Daley and Chief Warrant Officer Four Mike Gornick, were prepared for an "approach to minimums" (relying heavily on instruments).

With decreasing altitude, the fog thickened, changing from cold gray to a dull, eerie brown—like smoke from a gasoline fire.

Suddenly, there's a flash of green—treetops! From the passengers' perspective, their downward angle became an upward thrust as the pilots pulled out before making contact with a Carolina pine and becoming the big news in tomorrow's headlines.

The passengers—a composite team made up of Golden Knights from all sections of the team, became deathly quiet. Each man's

Hiller Porter that crashed in 1968, injuring several members of the team.

thoughts were his own as the green pinetops faded back into the fog. Expressions were serious. One man was talking to Jesus, while another muttered something that struck a nerve in all of them: "Silk Hope, man," he mumbled.

Sixteen years earlier, on March 8, 1973, 11 members of the Knights' Gold Demonstration Team, both pilots and the crew chief crashed their C-47 airplane in a muddy field near the farming community of Silk Hope, North Carolina, less than an hour's drive from Raleigh. They were headed for the first show of the 1973 season in Overland Park, Kansas—a show they never made. Within an hour after takeoff, or about 9:10 a.m., their plane was seen by a farmer's wife in a "spiraling nose dive." Within seconds, the hopes, dreams and lives of 14 Golden Knights were ended.

The '73 Crash remains fixed in the minds of all team members. Besides being a terrible tragedy of young lives, it also points to the most significant hazard faced by these Golden Knight teams. "The greatest danger in the sport of parachuting," explains Sergeant Jeff Steele, current Gold Team member, "isn't jumping, but getting to altitude. Most airplane crashes occur during takeoffs and landings, and the Golden Knights' aviation section conducts more takeoffs and landings than any other aviation section in the Army. After all,'' says Steele, ''the team essentially uses their aircraft as a jump platform which, after the jumpers depart, must land so its passengers can board for another one-way flight.''

Throughout their long history of landings and takeoffs, however, the Knights have experienced only two other airplane crashes in which team members were involved, neither of which were aircraft organic to the team. The C-123 which crashed in 1961, was an Air Force cargo plane. The single-engine Fairchild Hiller which crashed in 1968, was a contract plane.

''We went down to Wilmington that day before the show in a helicopter that was suppose to be our jump platform,'' John Hollis said. ''That night at a big reception with the Thunderbirds, they volunteered their cargo ship, and we say 'Hey, that'd be ideal!' We were all going to go out (the ramp) holding on to one another.''

Hollis said he and the team photographer, Bob Turner, were sitting up front, facing the bulkhead. After liftoff, the plane stalled out and began falling backward, tail first. Turner and five TV cameramen were standing up, taking pictures out of the back of the plane.

''I told Turner, 'you'd better sit down 'cause this thing's coming in,'' Hollis explained, shaking his head and looking at the floor as if he could see it happening again. ''Bout the time he sat down and got his seatbelt fastened up... well, we hit. And it just catapulted him out of his seat and slammed him into the bulkhead. The floor came right up to where my reserve was pressed against my face and my knees were around my ears. The crew chief just fell back down in the cockpit. Then I heard all these wires cracking and could smell gas and everything. And I said, 'well, this is it. I'm going.' I heard Bob McDonnell screaming but couldn't do anything. My back was broken. He was pinned in under the wing for 20 or 30 minutes...and... and it was burning.''

Hollis credits his rescuers with not only saving his life but making it possible for him to return to jumping. He said he was dragged from his seat to the stretcher by his parachute harness which decompressed the fractures in his lower vertebrate. Bob McDonnell, when he was finally freed from the wreckage, refused to allow them to transport him to the hospital until all of his teammates were out of the plane. Unknown to him, Turner was already dead, as were the crew chief, one of the pilots and two of the civilian TV cameramen.

Following the crash, the team took on several temporaries until those injured in the crash could return to their jumping duties. By then, however, the Army authorized the team to increase in size, so most of the temporaries were kept. When the team was at its supposed "weakest point" right after the crash, its real strengths began to show. Despite their losses, the team continued to perform and compete, to accomplish their mission with the most important resource available to them at the time—dedication. Tribulation, after all, brings about perseverance.

Seven years later, another crash occurred in Zephyrhills, Florida, January 30, 1968. This one wouldn't leave any fatalities but some team members were severely injured. Then Sergeant First Class Bobby "Spider" Wrenn was one of the injured.

"We were using this Hiller porter (single-engine plane), testing it to see if the Army would want to buy it." Wrenn said, using hand gestures to show how the plane crashed, "We were coming in for a landing, and we hit and hit hard and the tail wheel broke off. When it did that, it shot the plane up in the air about 500 feet and it just stalled out...came back down...FLAP...like a pancake. I was kneeling in the door and it threw me out under the wing."

Like Hollis, Wrenn suffered several cracked vertebrate. He also received a broken leg, two broken ribs and several lacerations. Despite his injuries, however, he refused to stay hospitalized and miss out of his teammates' record attempts. From his stretcher on the drop zone, he recorded the Knights taking 87 of the 128 existing world records. Wrenn was also back on his feet and jumping again in only a few months. He was so much like Hollis in his dedication and leadership, Wrenn became the team's first sergeant in 1977. Hollis and Wrenn are representative of the type of spirit that keeps the Golden Knights going, enabling the team to survive disasters and continue the mission.

Intermittent between the crashes of '61 and '68 and on through '71, were individual losses of team members killed in action in Vietnam. The Golden Knights consider themselves one big family, and the Vietnam War took several "family" members of the U.S. Army Parachute Team. But the names of those Knights who died in service to this country, as a popular country song says, are more than just names "upon a wall" at the Vietnam Memorial in Washington, D.C. or the team's Memorial Hall. Golden Knights killed in action in the Republic of Vietnam include the following:

SFC PHILLIP J. VANDERWEG
NOV 27, 1965

SFC BOBBY W. LETBETTER
NOV 26, 1966

SFC LEO N. KRYSKE
AUG 25, 1968

CPT JAMES R. DANIEL
JUNE 1, 1969

CW2 RICHARD V. PAWLAK
MARCH 3, 1970

CPT ALAN GARDNER
JUNE 7, 1970

MSG ED DeLUCA
JUNE 6, 1971

Bob Turner, the first team fatality, is also enshrined in the team's Memorial Hall, which is located at one end of the team's trophy room as a reminder of the cost of serving the nation. All seven of the team's parachute-related fatalities are also remembered. One of these fatalities, ironically, occurred only a few weeks before—almost as an omen to—the team's greatest disaster, the '73 Crash. Those Golden Knights who have died as a result of parachuting injuries include the following:

SSG ARNOLD A. ARRELLANO
JUNE 20, 1970

SP4 LEON D. WOLFE
FEBRUARY 18, 1973

SGT TIM A. ZEIGLER
JANUARY 21, 1980

SFC TOM JOHNSON
JUNE 15, 1980

SSG RICARDO GRANT
JUNE 18, 1982

SGT PRESTON L. KIRK
FEBRUARY 3, 1984

SSG PAUL E. JACKSON
MARCH 21, 1987

Another Golden Knight, Sgt. Gary L. Green, who died in a motorcycle accident at Fort Bragg, July 5, 1986, is also remembered in the Memorial Hall. But the greatest portion of that hall is dedicated to the 14 men who lost their lives all at once on that dreary morning in March 1973.

The C-47 (DC-3) twin-engine prop plane was of World War II vintage, but used by the Golden Knights because of its proven effectiveness as a jump platform. The team's use of non-standard Army aircraft presented several organizational maintenance problems, especially in getting repair parts. The Air Force had long since stopped using DC-3's.

In a quarterly report signed by the team commander, Captain Chris Needels, January 3, 1973, the "extreme age" of the aircraft was noted to have contributed to "frequent and major mechanical and avionics failures." The aircraft's constant use in supporting demos and training were also cited as potential problems by the commander. The next quarterly report would deal exclusively with the problem of meeting the team's show schedule with one less plane and 14 fewer Golden Knights. It would be three more years before the team would get the CY-7A Caribou to replace the C-47's. The Caribous would be replaced by the Fokker less than 10 years later. The 14 teammates killed in the '73 Crash could never be replaced.

On Wednesday, March 7th, the night before the crash, several members of the Gold Demonstration Team dropped by the various sport parachute clubs to say their seasonal "goodbyes." From now until November, they would be gone every weekend touring the country. Five members of the team were starting their very first demonstration season. Everyone was excited. Everyone was ready to go. Kansas was going to be a good show.

The morning of the crash started out like any other road trip morning with the usual preparations to meet "lobby," or appointed time to assemble in the team area. Husbands kissed their wives and hugged their babies, all expecting to see their families again in just a few days. Takeoff was scheduled for 8:30 a.m.

"I took Frank to work that morning, then I went to work," explained Joan Welch, wife of team leader—Sergeant First Class Francis Welch. "That's where I was when I heard about the crash."

Francis Welch was called "Frank" by his wife and "Whiskey Welch" by his teammates—a nickname he'd picked up in Vietnam after the phonetic designation of the first letter of his last name (Whiskey for the W in Welch). He'd been on the team since 1970. When his wife drove him to work that morning, they had no way of knowing he'd never see her or their four children again.

Approximately 40 minutes after leaving Fort Bragg, an explosion was said to have been heard by residents of the community of Silk Hope in Chatham County. That explosion was followed by a crash and another explosion. Pieces of wreckage were found more than a quarter-mile from the main fuselage, which appeared to have landed nose first. No skid marks were noted to indicate it had moved at all after impacting, splattering mud in all directions.

A large box of team literature lay opened in the middle of the muddy field—a field that still harbored stalks from last year's corn crop. Brochures telling the Golden Knight's story were being scattered by the winds when volunteer fireman and military investigators got to the scene. Several youngsters who'd gotten to the scene before military police blocked off the area, displayed to their friends the Golden Knight literature they'd picked up as

souvenirs.

News of the crash reached the team area back at Fort Bragg like a perilous Red Cross message. A crash? Who's hurt? Who's died? Who survived? Didn't anyone survive?! The entire team seemed to be in a state of shock. The Fayetteville OBSERVER noted the following day the "blank, uncomprehending stares" of team members who found it extremely hard to accept the loss of their teammates. Wives and children found the news more than shattering. Joan Welch got the news around lunch time from her brother, Joe Cranfield, who was also stationed at Fort Bragg at the time.

"I didn't officially get notified until later in the evening, and that drove me crazy," she said, her eyes fixed on her cigarette smoke. "At first they weren't sure which team went down because both teams had taken off about the same time, in the same direction. Then there were identification

The 1961 Crash at Wilmington, NC. .

problems. Pat Rice didn't get notified until something like one o'clock in the morning. When they did officially notify me, I went to my bedroom and that's where I stayed until my parents came.''

Despite the hundreds of phone calls coming into the team headquarters from all over the nation and the world, to most of the public, Frank Welch and the other 13 were only names in the news. To their families, they were husbands, fathers, sons and brothers. To their teammates, they were friends. They were family. (See box next page.)

Each man listed with a local address left a wife behind—an Army wife—a woman who supports her husband's devotion to his country and his unit and who's fully capable of being both mother and father in his absence. But for these Golden Knights' wives, the absence was permanent.

''You live with it,'' Joan said, tersely. ''You accept it. Mentally, you accept it. But inside you don't. After all these years, it still doesn't seem real. See, we not only loved each other, we actually liked each other. You just feel cheated, I guess. But I have a special place in my heart for all the Golden Knights. I always will because of the love that Frank had for the team and all the people."

Because of their children, Joan Welch decided to remain in Fayetteville, North Carolina, instead of moving closer to her family then living in New Jersey. North Carolina was home now. The North Carolina General

Assembly honored Joan Welch and the other wives through their husbands with a special resolution, part of which expressed the feelings of their families and teammates.

"Whereas others will succeed them, none can truly replace them in the minds and hearts of their families and citizens of this state and our nation," the resolution stated.

The team responded to the crash by taking jumpers from the three parachute clubs on Fort Bragg and calling back at least one "tryout" who'd been released from the team for ad-

ministrative reasons the year before. Master Sergeant Mark Shields was one of those the team recalled. Shields joined the team, along with others throughout the weeks following the crash. By consolidating these new team members with members of the competition team and headquarters section, the Knights were able to perform 132 demonstrations that year and continue their domination of parachute competitions, wining top honors in three international meets.

"Just when we were starting to get back on our feet," Shields said,

SFC FRANCIS WELCH	TEAM LEADER	FAYETTEVILLE, N.C.
SSGT JOSEPH PELTER	ASST. TEAM LEADER	FAYETTEVILLE, N.C.
SSGT JAMES RICE	JUMPER	FORT BRAGG, N.C.
SSGT JOSEPH BARBARICK	JUMPER	TERRE HAUTE, IND.
SGT MICHAEL BUCKLEY	JUMPER	FRANNINGTON, MASS.
SGT EDWARD PARRISH	JUMPER	SPRING VALLEY, CALIF.
SP5 MICHAEL WASLEY	JUMPER	FAYETTEVILLE, N.C.
PFC PAUL ALBRITTON	JUMPER	FAYETTEVILLE, N.C.
SSGT CECIL DAVIS	JUMPER	FAYETTEVILLE, N.C.
SSGT RAYMOND KINSER	JUMPER	SPRINGFIELD, MO.
SSGT ROBERT WOLFE	JUMPER	RADNER, PA.
CW3 RICHARD DEL CONTE	PILOT	FAYETTEVILLE, N.C.
CW2 RODNEY PEASE	CO-PILOT	MASSAPEQUA, N.Y.
SSGT BARTLEY BULLINGTON	CREW CHIEF	FAYETTEVILLE, N.C.

"DoD shut us down."

In late summer 1973, at the height of the energy crisis and end of the Vietnam War, the Department of Defense stopped all performances by all three services' demonstration teams. Inflation, Congressional spending cuts, fuel conservation— all these were factors leading to shutting down the teams. Congress saw no need for aerial demonstration teams and saw fit to "axe" them all at the same time. But during this same time, Congress had also ended the draft in support of an all-volunteer Army—a fine concept, but one that would require a bigger recruiting budget.

The fact that these aerial demonstrations were proven to enhance recruiting was indisputable. Keeping the demo teams as a recruiting tool was certainly a lot cheaper than returning to the draft or spicing up military benefits which Congress was already intent on reducing. Shields credits Captain Needels with saving the team by pointing out the recruiting potential. Besides, fuel for the USAPT was relatively low in cost, but if the Golden Knights were allowed to operate, so should the other teams. Having been shut down little more than a week, the teams were allowed to return to their demonstration schedules, but now with a more direct role in recruiting. The Army's other demo team—a helicopter team called the "Silver Eagles," ultimately suffered the most from this close inspection of the demo teams and was disbanded two years later in favor of one official aerial demonstration team for the Army—the Golden Knights.

In an October 1985 report which came to be called "the Kilcline Study" after its project officer, Vice Admiral Thomas J. Kilcline, it was noted the free publicity the services receive from the public performances of its demonstration teams amounted to about $7.25 million for one year. The report stated, "the teams are obviously an exceptional publicity asset." Then, in comparison to the other two teams, it said, "the Army's team performs four to five times as many shows as each of the jet teams in an effort to (reach) as many communities as possible."

Shields believes the Knights proved themselves cost effective enough to stay in business. And because the Army's team was allowed to stay in business, so was the Air Force and Navy teams. But all three teams would continue to be closely watched by budget analysts in Congress. Still, having survived three plane crashes and Congress, the Golden Knights were now able to return to doing what they do best—performing and competing in the name of the U.S. Army. More than ever, they would now have to prove themselves worth the money.

Following the missed approach into Simmons

Army Airfield that foggy January evening in 1989, Daley and Gornick made a successful landing at the Fayetteville Municipal Airport, earning endless applause from the men whose lives were in their skillful care. Daley explained that the steps the team took to ensure there'd be no more "Silk Hopes" were painstaking and thorough. Nonstandard Army aircraft now used by the team are maintained by veteran crew chiefs and maintenance crews and civilian maintenance teams contracted by the Army to guarantee the Knights' jump platforms would always be able to get them to altitude and stay out of tomorrow's headlines.

A DIFFERENT LOOK

The United States essentially had two armies until 1978—one for men and one for women. Women were excluded from a lot of job skills, particularly combat arms and combat support MOS's. But

changes in the system had already begun five years before the Women's Army Corps (the WAC's) was officially assimilated into the rest of the Army.

"Back in '73, while I was still in high school, I went to the recruiting station," explained world record-holder and world champion Cheryl Stearns. "I told them I wanted to be a Golden Knight, that I wanted to jump out of airplanes. They told me, 'No way. The Golden Knights are an all-male unit.' If I couldn't be a Knight, I wasn't interested in anything else they had to offer. But I said to myself, 'we'll see about that.'"

In December of the same year, the first female soldier graduated from Airborne School at Fort Benning, Georgia. More and more jobs began opening up to women. Meanwhile, Stearns—a Phoenix, Arizona native, was attending college on a tennis scholarship. Having been the state tennis champion her senior year of high

school, she could have gone to Arizona State University but opted for a smaller community college. When she wasn't in class or playing tennis, she was improving her skydiving skills—a sport she took up at the minimum allowed age of 16 with her parents' consent (as opposed to blessings).

William and Joan Stearns of Scottsdale, Arizona were less than enthusiastic about seeing their little girl jump from an airplane. But their daughter had always been independent and strong-willed, what some folks might call a tomboy.

"My friends were the type who played with Barbie dolls and made plans about becoming wives and having a bunch of kids," she said, grinning as she shook her head. "That wasn't for me. I tend to get bored real easily. Life has to be thrilling...challenging. I can't be tied down."

In addition to jumping, playing tennis and going to school, Stearns was working on a commercial pilot's license. In fact, by the time she was 20, she was a flight instructor. To her regret, she often had to choose between an opportunity to jump, which cost money, and flying, by which she paid her own way through school. She eventually earned an associate's, a bachelor's and a master's degree (the B.S. and M.S. were earned through Embry Riddle Aeronautical University).

"A friend of mine, Billy Ledbetter, challenged me a dollar a jump to shoot accuracy," she laughed as she pointed out some of the ways she supported her hobby. "I couldn't afford to lose 'cause I couldn't afford to pay the guy a dollar. So, I kind of had no choice but to become good in accuracy. As a matter of fact, I was pretty hot under a round canopy."

Stearns says she never even saw a square canopy until she jumped with one in 1975. By that time, she was flying for former Golden Knight Gene

Paul Thacker, who runs an airfield and drop zone near Raeford, North Carolina. Stearns heard about Thacker through a parachuting friend who was about to go to Raeford to train for the U.S. Parachute Team.

"I wrote Gene Paul a letter, explaining my qualifications as a pilot and jumper," she said. "He was very impressed by my letter and wrote me, inviting me to Raeford. He didn't tell me the only other woman pilot who'd worked for him had crashed one of his planes. He's like that."

Thacker, a former national Style & Accuracy champion, has been a godfather to a lot of novice skydivers and pilots, Stearns noted. His link with the Army Parachute Team is probably closer than any other former team member. Even though he no longer competes himself, he's brought up two sons, Tim and Tony, to be both pilots and competition parachutists. Not only did he help Stearns by giving her a

job, he helped train her as a jumper. And, more importantly, he was instrumental in getting her on the Golden Knights.

"When I first came to Raeford, I looked around me at the airfield and drop zone, and thought, I'm in seventh heaven," Stearns said. "All I had to do now was fly and jump. Then I found out the Golden Knights were based nearby at Fort Bragg, and that old desire to be a Knight came back. One day Gene Paul took me off to the side and told me the team was as interested in me as I was in them."

Former executive officer, Captain Chuck Whittle, and First Sergeant Bobby Wrenn, almost guaranteed Stearns that if she enlisted for Fort Bragg, they'd bring her on the team as a still photographer, then try her on the Style & Accuracy Team.

"Contractwise, all I was guaranteed was Fort Bragg," said Stearns. "All I had to do was graduate from basic training and become a soldier. My photography training was to be OJT (on the job training). I went to jump school right after I signed into the team.''

When she came to the team in April 1977, Stearns had 1,500 freefall parachute jumps, but she was shipped out to Fort Benning right away to become airborne qualified—to make five static line jumps and learn to be a paratrooper. By the time she returned, the team was preparing to leave for the nationals. She hadn't trained since January, but still gave a good effort at defending the overall national title she won at the '76 nationals when she was still a civilian.

Every female competitor at the '77 nationals had already learned to respect Stearns' competitive ability, but now that she was a Golden Knight, she would become someone to fear in competition, for such was the reputation of the team—to make the best even better. To competitors and spectators alike, one thing was certain—her feminine face stood out sharply from among the 11 masculine faces who were now her teammates. At the 1977 U.S. National Skydiving Championships, the world was introduced to a slightly different U.S. Army Parachute Team.

FIRST LADY OF SKYDIVING

Athletes don't have time to be bothered with the symptoms of a cold, particularly during a competition. And yet, those terrible muscle aches, the fever and that overall "blah" feeling were taking their toll on Cheryl Stearns during the '86 nationals. By this time, she had served two 3-year tours with the Army Parachute Team, 1977-1980 and 1982-1985. When she wasn't jumping these days, she was flying 737's for Piedmont Airlines. Each year, however, as was her custom, she came to the nationals to take home her usual quota of gold medals and take her place on the U.S. Parachute Team.

This year just wasn't going so well. She was turning the fastest times in style and getting dead centers in accuracy, but she was getting competition from

Cheryl Stearns at 1980 World Meet with teammates Maurice Fernandez and Cliff Jones (rear).

where she had least expected it. Her biggest competitors were not former teammates Terry Bennett Vares or Janice Captain, but a microscopic monster—a virus.

Each landing during the accuracy event caused her body to revolt against her, threatening to come apart. At least, it felt that way. She saw sparks before her eyes, felt weak in the knees and longed just to lay down in the shade and not get up. But she stayed in the competition. On her final approach in the sixth round of accuracy, Stearns blacked out only a 100-feet above the accuracy pit. She came to just as she was about to land—off target!

"I had just enough time to lay myself out 90 degrees, reaching for the target," she explained as she demonstrated, feet together, toes pointing and legs bent perpendicular to her body. "When I did that, my reserve slid over to one side where the hook was pressed against my hip. The full force of my weight landed on the reserve. I tried to move but couldn't. I thought my hip was broken for sure."

It wasn't broken, but badly bruised all the way to the bone. The injury to her hip affected her whole leg, rendering her crippled for several days. For the first time in 10 years, it appeared she was going to be out of the competition and not be on the U.S. Team.

"They (USPA officials) came to me and told me I could still get on the U.S. Team if I could only complete the final rounds with a good score," Stearns said. "I couldn't even walk, but I got some of the guys to help me chute up and carry me to the plane. When I landed, I had to concentrate on hitting the target and staying off my bad side."

Despite her injuries, she made the U.S. Team and traveled to Turkey for the world championships. Between the nationals and the world meet, Stearns

wasn't able to make any practice jumps because she wanted to allow her hip time to heal. Even without training, she took the gold medal in accuracy and second place overall behind her former Golden Knight teammate, Terry Bennett Vares. Stearns' determination to stay in the competition at the nationals paid off with the U.S. making a near clean-sweep of the women's Style & Accuracy competition.

Stearns' reputation as a competitor is phenomenal. Since 1974, the first year she competed, she has been the women's overall national champion 11 times. She's been on a U.S. Parachute Team every year since 1976, winning the gold medal in style and the overall title at the '78 world meet and the gold medal in accuracy at both the '82 and '86 world meets. In 1980, she dropped to third place overall at the world meet, but has since maintained a second place overall finish. Her ultimate goal, she says, is to make a clean sweep, winning both style and accuracy and therefore the overall title.

In addition to winning gold medals, Stearns is a world record holder. The same year she became the first female Golden Knight world champion in 1978, she broke the world record for day and night accuracy jumps by scoring 43 consecutive hits during the day and 23 consecutive hits at night. In 1987, she didn't just break, but shattered the women's record for the number of jumps made in a 24-hour period.

"The men's record at that time was 240 jumps in 24 hours," she said. "The women's record was only 79. Russell Fish and I decided to see if we could break the record. We wound up averaging a jump every five minutes, 23 seconds."

Logistical support for this record attempt was provided by sponsors who were curious to see if the old record—the men's record—could be broken. There was never any doubt that Stearns could break the women's record. Throughout the long ordeal, three planes supported them, along with parachute packers on the ground.

"We jumped at 2,000 feet," she explained. "I landed, had about 30 yards to run over to my next chute and get it on. They gave us snack foods like carrot sticks with peanut butter on them and sips of water. We had portapotties there, but during the last 10 hours, I didn't even get a chance to go to the bathroom."

When 24 hours of back-to-back jumping were over, Stearns and Fish set a new record— one to be shared by men and women, for both made 255 jumps in 24 hours.

Stearns is making no plans on retiring from the sport. At 34, she jokingly says she has "lots of good years left in her." She may wonder, at times, what the recruiter who told her she couldn't be a Golden Knight might say to her successes in a supposed all-male sport like parachuting, much less her history-making assignment to the U.S. Army Parachute Team.

"I was recruited to the team," she said. "But it was what I wanted. All my life I had wanted to be a world champion. The Golden Knights made that happen for me. And those guys were great, too. Everybody was like a brother. They took me under their wings...I mean, no one questioned my jumping ability. But I didn't know anything about parachute demonstrations or giving a high school presentation. They taught me those things."

Until Karen Sellers— the first female demonstrator, came on the team, Stearns served a dual role whenever the competition schedule allowed. She performed in aerial demonstrations in her hometown of Phoenix and even jumped with the American flag at the Statue of Liberty in New York City. The team tried to show her face around the country as

SGT Cheryl Stearns

commander, Lieutenant Colonel Kirk Knight, the invitation to female soldiers to join the Golden Knights is always open. Team members are even encouraged to actively recruit women to try out for the team. Though another Cheryl Stearns isn't expected, the search for her is never-ending.

Stearns continues to serve the Army through the Kentucky National Guard as a staff sergeant. She flies for U.S. Air (who absorbed Piedmont Airlines in 1989) now, but never misses a chance to compete in the U.S. nationals and takes her customary position on the U.S. Team. Each winter, she rejoins her teammates in Yuma, Arizona for the Golden Knights annual winter training. Her presence there is an inspiration to every female on the team, who look to her as the beginning for women soldiers and gave them a chance to prove they, too, can be included among the best in the Army.

much as possible in order to attract other female jumpers and soldiers to become interested in joining the team.

Although scores of female soldiers have served on the team in supporting roles in supply, administration, operations and public affairs, since 1977—a year before men and women were officially joined in the same Army—only 13 women have served on the Army Parachute Team as demonstrators or competitors.

According to team

SGT Karen Sellers, Demonstrator

These 14 freefall-qualified women soldiers have served or are currently serving on the U.S. Army Parachute Team. Not all serve the team as jumpers; that is, as demonstrators or competitors. Some, like Perry and Wilson, who only recently completed their accelerated freefall training, make use of their experience and appreciation of the sport in order to better support their teammates on the demonstration and competition teams.

SGT Terry Bennett Vares,
Demonstrator and Competitor

SGT Annie Gross Gallagher,
Demonstrator

SGT Doreen Connally,
Demonstrator and Competitor

SGT Janice Captain,
Demonstrator and Competitor

SGT Jeanne Stoegbauer Lasher
Demonstrator and Competitor

SGT Cristy Kauble,
Demonstrator

SSGT Maria White, Rigger-Jumper

SGT Cathleen Sherritt, Demonstrator

SGT Elisa Feldt, Demonstrator

SPC Dianna Belcher, Rigger-Jumper

SPC Laurel Perry, Photographer   SGT Laura Wilson, Journalist

An unidentified Golden Knight guides in on the target at an airshow in Wilmington, N.C. with the POW-MIA flag trailing behind. Wilmington, which is only 40 miles from the author's hometown, was the site of the first team disaster. The same month R.C. Murray was starting the first grade, the U.S. Army Parachute Team experienced its first tragedy when the C-123 cargo plane in which they were flying crashed on takeoff. The team's photographer, SGT Bob Turner, died in that crash.

Image Makers 1988: (from left) Tom Shriver, Kevin Oleksy, Bob Finn, R.C. Murray and John Spann.

1990 Media Relations: (back row, from left) SGT Laura Wilson, Donna Council, and SPC Laurel Perry. (front row, from left) SGT Joe Belcher and SSGT R.C. Murray.

Stearns still on target (1990).

Above and next page: The Golden Knights' trophy room, which only houses about 60 percent of the trophies, medals, plaques, cups, etc., is a favorite stop for tourists visiting Fort Bragg.

Black and Gold Demonstration team members.

THE IMAGE MAKERS

He gently set the phone back on its receiver, resisting the temptation to slam it home. Sergeant Joe Belcher was a little upset by something. His whole face seemed to glow a brilliant shade of red right on up into his thinning hairline. When asked what was troubling him, he looked around the team's media relations office as if searching for the right words to express his frustration.

"You know what she told me?" He finally said with a distinct Southern twang, "She said the only time their paper was interested in a story about the military was when we put a plane in the dirt!"

After a few calming words from his supervisor, a cup of strong Army coffee and a stroll around the room, Belcher returned to his desk, picked up the phone and resumed calling the press for an upcoming air show. It was his job to generate as much publicity as possible for the Knights' demonstration teams by contacting every newspaper, radio and television station and local magazine in the area surrounding the show. Belcher knew insults from anti-military reporters and news editors were not uncommon, although casual indifference was more typical. Still, he wouldn't let one insult prevent him from doing his job.

As publicity is the very lifeblood of the Army Parachute Team, Belcher's job is no easy one. According to his

1989 World Champion 8-way Relative Work Team at the U.S. Nationals Skydiving Championship over Muskogee, Oklahoma.

predecessors, it never has been. During 30 years of contacting press, taking photographs and writing news releases, their office has grown from one photojournalist in 1960, to its present strength of two press coordinators (one of whom doubles as a writer), an Army and a civilian photographer/darkroom technician and an editor/supervisor. The office itself has changed its name from "Public Information Office" to "Information Office to Media Relations." Its mission, however, hasn't changed at all.

The team's mission statement, even when it was still the STRAC Team, was unclear in its definition of the qualities—the image—expected of a team member. That image, after all, was what set the team apart from other units. Undefined standards couldn't be allowed to continue, so the **PIO—Don Kidd—** established them rather formally in a news release in 1960:

"The Army Team jumper is a paratrooper...who has hundreds of parachute jumps...He is one of the healthiest and most alert men in the world. His selection to the team depends upon many factors: he must be an expert parachutist, must have the qualities necessary to live very closely with his teammates for long periods of time without creating friction or dissension, and must be able to represent the Army as an 'Ambassador of Good Will.'

"He must exemplify the best of the Army in personal appearance, personality, behavior and reaction toward others. He must be highly motivated to jump and perform aerial maneuvers, must be capable of withstanding long, grueling practice sessions and road shows, must demonstrate an unfailing good nature, and must be able to express himself well on all subjects pertinent to the Army on radio and television shows and in personal appearances."

"I articulated things about the team that I felt would enhance the team's image," Kidd explained. "It was my job to do that. Those guys had enough to do with all the jumping and performing. It was up to me to tell the public about the team and what they did."

Kidd originally enlisted in the Army in December 1942. He fought through World War II as an infantryman in the Pacific Campaign, then left the Army in February 1946 to sell life insurance and foreign sports cars. He returned to active duty after 10 years break in service to fill a yearning to "put back on a uniform." He was serving special duty from a psychological warfare unit on Fort Bragg to the XVIII Airborne Corps Public Affairs Office when Brigadier General Stilwell realized his parachute team wasn't going to get anywhere without publicity. Kidd was command-directed by the chief of staff to report special-duty from his already special-duty assignment to the STRAC Team, where he was to "stay" as far as Stilwell was concerned.

Kidd considers his greatest achievement in the short time he was actually with the team before being sent overseas to France, to be an article called, "A Brief History of Army Sport Parachuting," which was published in the Congressional Record. Another of his more crowning works of promotion for the Knights was in the form of a memo which he wrote on behalf of the team, after he was no longer part of the team.

Knowing their former PIO was stationed in France as the team prepared to leave for Laferte-Gaucher, France, in July 1961, Jim Perry requested Kidd be attached to the team upon their arrival. Perry's request was honored through some high-ranking channels. A Pentagon message came into Kidd's modest public affairs office requesting him by name, much to the dismay of his supervisor—a young captain who was more than a little surprised by the VIP journalist in his office.

Once notified of his mission, Kidd sat down and jotted off a memo to the Chief Public Affairs Officer—a Navy admiral, requesting support for the team. After identifying himself and his role with the team, Kidd briefly discussed the careers of each member of the team, beginning with **Colonel William P. Grieves**—the team leader of this U.S. Team, and several other competitions involving the Army Team members. Grieves, who was assigned to XVIII Airborne Corps Artillery, was tasked by Stilwell to support the Army Parachute Team logistically, though he often lent his support personally by going on the road with the team.

Kidd summed up the team by saying they portrayed "the red-blooded American male, a manly image of the Army paratrooper, the Army athlete and the American soldier generally." He then admitted his limited ability to support the team as he felt they should be supported upon their arrival, but noted that if he was in a position to do so, he would "ensure the following things were accomplished for them." (See box, next page.)

The determined Army sergeant overwhelmed the admiral. As requested, this obviously special team was met with an informal welcome by an officer of equal rank to Colonel Grieves, plus transportation, both ground and air, to be used by the team for travel and training. Everything Kidd asked for, he received and then some. His ability to express himself for the benefit of the Army Parachute Team made him an indispensable asset to the team's mission. Throughout the team's history, others who served as image makers became just as invaluable. **Phillip C. Miller** was one of them.

Like Kidd, Miller was a World War II veteran. He even spent time as a prisoner of war. He was also a Korean War veteran. Miller was the only member of the team to wear a Combat Infantryman's Badge with a star, signifying involvement in two different conflicts, and he was the only team member up to that time to have made a combat jump. Following a reduction in force (RIF), Miller gave up his battlefield commission and came to the team in 1963 as a sergeant first class. He became qualified as an internationally rated judge, and even helped plan and direct the world championships in 1964. During his tenure with the Golden Knights, Miller served as a demonstrator and competitor, and he took control of the publicity department in order to record the history of the team up to 1965.

His article, "History of United States Participation in Modern Day Competition Parachuting" was published in SKYDIVING and PARACHUTIST magazines, as well as various transla-

tions in German, French and other European and Eastern block magazines. By name, he listed the all-Army team that competed in the 2nd Adriatic Cup in 1959: **Colonel William P. Grieves, Major Merrill Sheppard, Lieutenant Paul Merrick, Sergeant First Class Alva English, Specialist Five Danny Byard, Specialist Four Loy B. Brydon** and **Private First Class James Pearson.**

"With the advent of the U.S. Army's encouragement of competitive parachuting, a major source of highly proficient sport parachutists soon emerged," he wrote.

About a year after completing the history project, Miller added another first to his credit by becoming the first member of the Army Parachute Team to retire from the Army while a member of the team, a noteworthy accomplishment and one that made a good story for the news media. Finding a good story and getting it to the public through the media was

1. An informal welcome should be arranged at planeside and an officer of equal rank with Col. Grieves should head the group. They should be guests at an informal dinner or cocktail party at one of the officers or non-commissioned officers mess in this area.

2. The welcome and party should be publicized in local press and their arrival here should go out on the wire services for stateside consumption.

3. Local photo processing facilities (military) should be notified as soon as possible to give all necessary support for reasonable quantity picture requirements.

4. The group should be asked to give a demonstration at Camp des Loges for SHAPE (Supreme Headquarters Allied Powers Europe), and EUCOM (European Command), VIP's, plus local press.

5. Local information offices should be asked to help in the preparation of suitable press kits for handouts to French and other press media reps. Translations of bio sheets, poop sheets on the Army team and other info is a prime consideration and greatly facilitates our getting maximum publicity from this event."

and always has been the mission of the Knights' image makers.

Sergeant Major (retired) **Dave Goldie** came to the team's information office shortly after the '73 Crash, which gave him the initial public relations mission of repairing any damage to the team's image that the crash might have caused. He was also an instrumental voice in promoting changes within the team through the publicity he got for the team. For example, the team's executive officer, **Captain Chuck Whittle**, was looking for support in getting the team the Caribou to replace the C-47's and the new square canopies to replace the Para-Commander. He got his support through news releases from the information office which got the attention of people who were able to do something about it.

Goldie also exercised his public relations expertise by offering strong advice to bring younger soldiers and females onto the team through tryouts. By no means was he suggesting the standards themselves needed to be changed. A two-year minimum time in service was already in place, but few tryouts were ever chosen with less than six years in the Army. For that reason, most team members were not only senior as far as time in service, most were in their late 20's and early 30's. To more effectively attract younger people into the Army, he argued, the team needed younger jumpers.

Goldie's recommendations met with some resistance on the team, many of whom felt he should stick to news releases and photos and leave personnel matters to the tryout cadre. But his advice was eventually accepted and implemented. In 10 years time, the average age of a Golden Knight dropped nearly three years, with the older team members serving on the competition team, where experience counts most and the younger team members on the demonstration teams who have the most direct contact with the public. And, of course, female soldiers began showing up in team lineups, in headquarters at first, then the competition team and finally the demonstration teams.

Changes in the team's makeup and appearance and an ever-changing public opinion of the military required changing tactics by the team's image makers. Generating press for the team was no longer a concern for individual demonstrations or competitions, but a day-by-day operation, requiring a full staff of public relations experts.

Sergeant First Class Bob Finn had nearly 10 years on the team when he took over the team's information office.

"The team had a news clipping service when I came down to IO in January 1988," Finn said. "Any news article anywhere in the country that contained the words 'Golden Knight' was clipped and sent to the team. After some personnel changes in the office, our monthly clipping service bill increased tenfold.''

Finn never claimed to be an expert in the public affairs field. But he knew who the experts were. He brought one of the team's freefall photographers, **Staff Sergeant Tom Shriver**, into the information office, along with an Army broadcast journalist, **Sergeant Kevin Oleksy**. They and another Army photographer, **Staff Sergeant John Spann**, who worked as a darkroom technician, and a writer attached to the team special duty, generated so much press in 1988, they decided to change their office name from information office to media relations.

''The Media Relations office deals directly with newspapers, television and radio stations...you name it,'' explained Shriver, who's now assigned as an Army photographer in Hawaii. ''The Golden Knights are unique in that they can talk directly to Department of the Army Public Affairs without going through channels.''

''The name 'information office' left an image of a booth or something that people could come to if they wanted some information on the team,'' Oleksy added. ''But you don't wait for someone to come to you requesting information. You go to them. That's why we changed the name.''

Other changes occurred within the office that not only enhanced their productivity, but earned the respect of their teammates. Since the '70's, 10-minute movies about the team had been contracted out by the team to civilian media firms who knew little about the team and who usually produced a movie reflecting this deficit. In 1989, the Knights' media relations office wrote the script for their own movie, contacted and coordinated with the Army's Combat Pictorial Detachment (CPD) at Fort Meade, Maryland to shoot the team in action. They then supervised CPD's editing and production of the finished product. The result was a 12-minute movie and various 30-, 60-and-90-second Public Service Announcement videos (PSA) which told the Golden Knight story in more detail than ever before.

The media relations office or ''MR,'' as they refer to themselves, have no qualms about using talents where they find them. Through the years, various artistic talents have surfaced among team members. These talents, for the most part, were never used to their full potential by the image makers until **Sergeant Bill Jackson** painted a lithograph for the Black Team and offered it to the team for reproduction and distribution. He has since been called upon to paint a second print—this one a special limited edition print that helped the team to celebrate its 30th birthday. More recently, Jackson's expertise in layout and design was used by MR in designing a new team

It's called a "Pendulum" or "down plane." Three jumpers performing Canopy Relative Work (CRW pronounced "crew") stack their canopies, forming a tri-plane. The lower jumper pulls down hard on his left or right toggle while turning upside down, his legs entwined with the middle jumper's legs.

brochure, which included computer-enhanced illustrations of team maneuvers drawn by Jackson.

The image makers of today not ony have ''more irons in the fire'' than their predecessors, they have more competition as well. Every major unit in the Army now has a public affairs office. For that reason, column inches in Army publications that used to be reserved for the Army Parachute Team are now more competitive. A Golden Knight demonstration is no longer news in itself because the team has performed more than 6,000 aerial demonstrations. Winning a competition is no longer big news either because the Knights are always winning something. To compete with division-size public affairs offices for space on the pages of ARMY TIMES or SOLDIERS magazine, a story about the team has to be demonstratively different than anything ever written about the team before.

If competition within

Staff Sergeant Doug Lane prepares to catch the American flag as Sergeant Dan Molesky approaches the target in front of the Market Square Courthouse in downtown Fayetteville, N.C., hometown of the Golden Knights; however, any town in the country is home to the men and women of the Army Parachute Team, better known to the world as simply, the Golden Knights.

Sergeant Jeff Steele reaches for the 14-inch wooden baton passed in mid-air during freefall.

Army publications isn't enough, sheer indifference is often the response from the civilian media, who look with suspicion at anything the military does. Television is usually more receptive than newspapers, perhaps because of the visual image team freefall footage can add to a news broadcast. Radio stations are still willing to host a Golden Knight because team members have earned a reputation of ''talking a good show.'' The wire services still grab up major competition results, but with abbreviated conclusions. And hometown papers still seek feature stories about team members.

There are more than a few newspapers and TV stations, as well as radio stations, however, who are beyond ''suspect'' of the military to being totally anti-military. These ''ambulance chasers,'' says Belcher, have no interest in anything about the military unless the reporting of which would reflect adversely

Top: Hawaii exit shot with a fish-eye lens.
Bottom: Opening ceremonies of 1980 Winter Olympics at Lake Placid, N.Y.

on the military. For example, a soldier who saves the life of a drowning child might make the B Section of the local paper, but a soldier arrested for anything would be sure to embellish the front page.

When 10 Golden Knights went to Seoul, South Korea to perform in the opening ceremonies for the 1988 Summer Olympics, the media response to their participation was lukewarm, to say the least. That, is until a Republic of Korea (ROK) parachutist had a malfulction during a training jump and was seen landing in the empty stadium. He wasn't hurt, but a rumor shot back to Fort Bragg via the wire services that he was killed and that he was a Golden Knight. Suddenly, everybody was interested in what the Army team was doing in Seoul.

The phones in MR went wild. What was his name? How many jumps did he have? How old was the equipment he

Bi-plane formation with American flag over Mt. Rushmore (1985).

American flag in freefall (from left, sergeants Mason Gallagher, Roger Jutras and Fernando Arrufat).

was using? The winds were too high, right? Was he a chronic user of alcohol or any other drug? Every question was a leading question, and no one would accept the disappointing news that no one had died.

"What?!" quipped a sleepy but obviously aggravated Captain Glenn Bangs when he was awakened by a phone call to confirm or deny the rumors. Although the team's operations officer, as a former world champion, Bangs was in Seoul to participate in the opening ceremonies.

When it was finally confirmed through the phone call that Bangs and all nine other Golden Knights were sleeping soundly until the phone disturbed him, the interest in the team's participation in the Olympics began to cool down. Demonstrating their ability to seize an opportunity, though, the team's image makers quickly fanned the flames of interest by explaining just how and why the team was at the

Sergeant First Class Mark Shields lands center field with NFL flag at XVII Super Bowl.

Sergeant First Class Mike Sweeney practices jumping in football for XVII Super Bowl.

Olympics. And although the ''good news'' about American soldiers participating in the Olympics didn't compare to American deaths abroad, the story found an audience at last.

The unfailing good nature with which Don Kidd wrote was a prerequisite to portraying the proper image of a Golden Knight—the most important prerequisite for the job he held as the team's image maker. Therefore, indifferent, even hostile press are always treated respectfully. After all, the image makers not only expound the image of the Golden Knights, they must reflect that image themselves more than anyone else on the team. These Golden Knight promoters must deal directly and effectively with those most capable of propagating or destroying that image—the media.

Staff Sergeant Doug Lane eyes the target in front of Liberty Memorial in Kansas City, Kansas, as Sergeant Phil Peyton prepares to catch the American flag.

An unidentified Golden Knight drops in on the capital of Vermont.

Sergeant First Class Gary Mohler gets a perfect 0.0 score after placing his left heel dead center on a target not much bigger than a silver dollar.

Double-Spider formation.

109

Bi-pole Flake formation.

Sergeant First Class Tom Welgos prepares to "turn points" during a training jump for Style competition.

Tri-plane formation with
American flag approaching
St. Louis Arch.

Opposite page: 1989 8-way Relative Work World Champions—Sergeants First Class Andy Gerber and Chris Wagner, Staff Sergeants Jim Coffman, Scott Rhodes, Charlie Brown and Paul Rafferty and Sergeants Craig Girard and Willie Lee—demonstrate their championship form for team Alternate/Video Photographer Sergeant Todd Lorenzo.

Above: Sergeant Chuck Lackey, 1989 U.S. National Style & Accuracy champion, sets up his final approach on the target—a five centimeter disk.

Opposite page: 8-way "RW" Team exit from F27 Fokker.

Above: 1981 4-way Relative Work World Champions— Staff Sergeants Glenn Bangs and Mike Deveault, Specialist Five Bob Finn, Sergeant Andy Gerber and Specialist Five Mark Gabriel (team alternate not shown) show off their championship teamwork.

Opposite page: Gold ring of
Niagara Falls, N.Y.

Left: Bi-plane formation with
American flag.
Near Mt. Rushmore (1989).

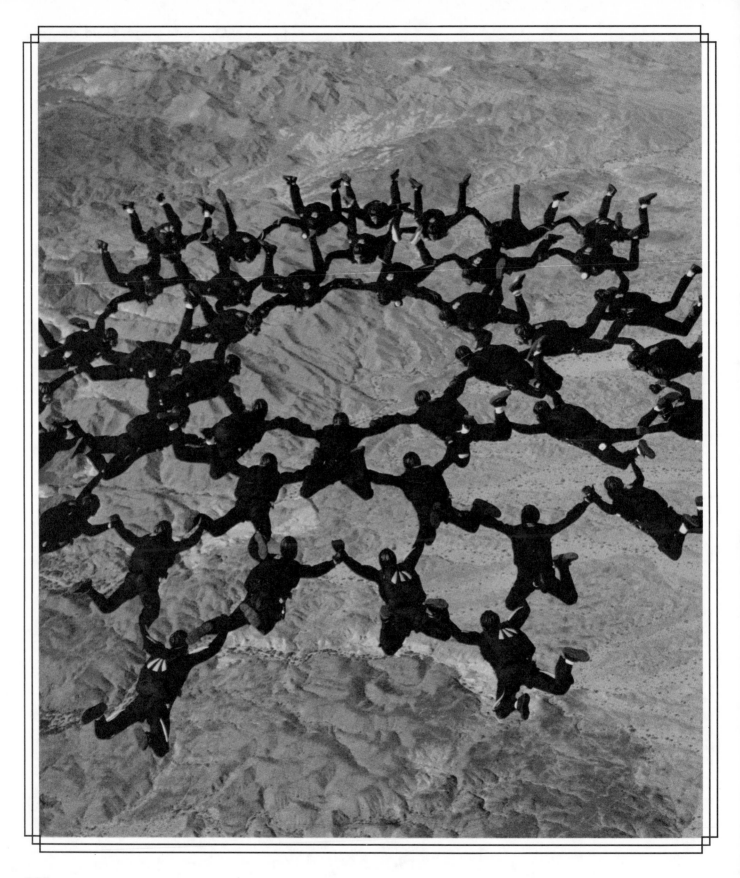

Opposite page: A military world record was set in February, 1989, when 45 Golden Knights jumped from the tailgate of a C-130 at 16,000 feet. An 18-man base was formed using an 8-way formation. The entire forma- tion was completed in 46 seconds and held for another 22 seconds.

Above: Gold ring over Sidney, Australia (1986).

Opposite page: Staff Sergeant Dave Haberkorn under canopy with American flag prepares to land behind the Lincoln Memorial as part of the opening ceremonies of the 1989 Presidential Inauguration.

Above: Gold ring over St. Louis Arch.

126

Air shows are fun and a learning experience. At the Cleveland Air Show, 1989, Golden Knight Staff Sergeant Jason Davis gets help packing his parachute from Dennis Bartow II, Aaron Bartow and Colin Brown.

Publisher Dennis Bartow with sons Dennis II, Aaron and Nathan Bartow and friend, Colin Brown, pose proudly with a "Knight."

Top left: Aaron Bartow, future Knight?

Bottom: Atop the wing of a Navy plane, Aaron looks skyward at the Golden Knights' performance, with a helpful Navy training pilot.

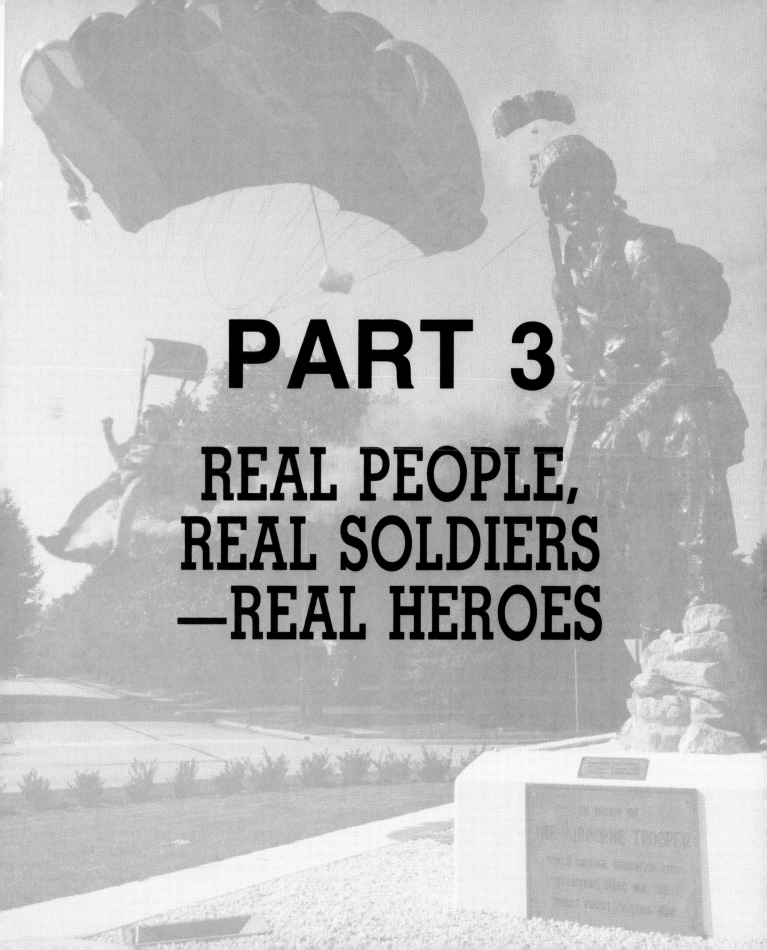

PART 3

REAL PEOPLE,
REAL SOLDIERS
—REAL HEROES

PART 3

REAL PEOPLE, REAL SOLDIERS —REAL HEROES

Despite having severe burns over most of his body, **Bob McDonnell** refused to allow his rescuers to use their medevac helicopter to take him to the hospital as long as his teammates were still aboard the C-123 that crashed in Wilmington, North Carolina in 1961. His teammate, **Doug Runnels**, risked his own life by assisting medical and fire department personnel in evacuating the burning plane of all passengers. For their selflessness in an emergency situation, both men were later awarded the Soldiers' Medal. And yet, selfless behavior appears to be the norm among members of the Golden Knights, past and present.

While off duty in downtown Fayetteville, North Carolina one spring day in 1989, **Sergeant Jeff Steele** spotted a man fleeing from Fayetteville police. The man had an apparent advantage of distance from his pursuers and it seemed obvious he would get away. That is, until Steele joined in the pursuit. The accused burglar jumped a fence and ran across a vacant lot to escape police. Steele stayed with him. During the chase, Steele saw the man deliberately try to hide a handgun as he and police were closing in on him. Exhausted and unable to lose the fleet-footed "plain clothes cop" he thought was on his heels, the fugitive was finally tackled by Steele and a city policeman. Even when he saw the gun, Steele said he never considered the risks involved, only that his help was needed. For providing that help and taking those risks, Steele was honored with a Liberty Bell Award by the Fort Bragg commander, Lieutenant General Carl Stiner.

Between McDonnell and Steele in the team's long history, there are more "heroes," too numerous to mention. The caliber of soldiers who have served on this team has always been the highest found throughout the Army.

Many of the early team members such as **Perry, Hollis** and **Miller** were highly decorated veterans of World War II and Korea. Perry and Miller earned battlefield commissions in the Korean Conflict. Original team members, **Pete Feliciano** and **Danny Byard**, went on to Officer Candidate School, while teammates, **Jerry Bourquin, Coy McDonald** and **Dick Fortenberry** went on to Warrant Officer Flight School, an indication of the confidence the Army had in these individual soldiers. **Sherman Williford**, an E-4 on the Army Parachute Team in the early '60's, is a brigadier general (promotable) today.

Throughout the '60's and the Vietnam years, former Golden Knights continued to prove themselves "the epitome of the United States Army soldier" by serving as infantry "grunts," medics and other supporting roles such as aviators. In 1971, **Chief Warrant Officer Michael Novosel** received this nation's highest award—the Medal of Honor, for his valor and gallantry as a "dust-off" pilot in Vietnam.

But these men are just some of the members of the team who've shone brightly because of their willingness to risk their lives, and more importantly, surrender their personal egos in order to accomplish a military mission. Real soldiers are not Rambos fighting as a one-man Army. Real soldiers are those nameless young faces in the trenches awaiting an enemy attack. Real soldiers are those truck drivers moving needed supplies up and down roads known to be mined, or where the enemy lays in ambush. Real soldiers are individually competent and unified by their common mission. Real soldiers are a team, and the Golden Knights are their representatives— men and women who firmly believe it's imperative to set a proper example for young people and explain to them why it's a privilege and an honor to be a soldier.

The men and women who have worn the black and gold uniform of the Golden Knights are not simply names and faces of performers and competitors who have appeared in the news. They're real people. They're real soldiers. Most of all, they're real heroes. They're not heroes because of what they've done or what they do. They're heroes because of what they are. Each Golden Knight possesses the special drive for excellence which sets him or her apart. For this reason, the Golden Knights are special because of the people themselves. The remainder of this chapter is dedicated to the "typical" Golden Knight.

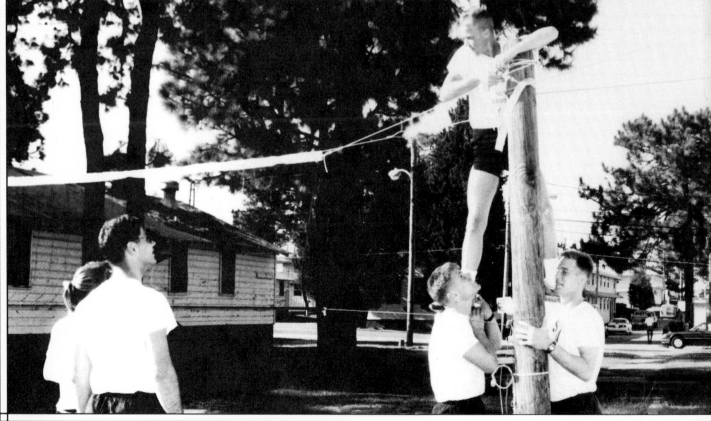

Tryouts are held annually at Fort Bragg. Prospective Golden Knights are continually evaluated for their soldierly attitudes, physical fitness and jumping skills throughout the six-week training period.

THE BLACK DEMONSTRATION TEAM

"It was the jump of a lifetime," said **Sergeant First Class Earl Eckbold**, former team leader of the Black Team. "In fact, it was the premier jump in the 30-year history of the Army Parachute Team."

The jump Eckbold referred to took place at precisely 4:42 p.m., January 18, 1989. It was a jump setting a number of firsts for the Golden Knights and the sport of parachuting.

"This was the first time this team has participated in a presidential inauguration," said Eckbold. "And it was the first time anyone has ever parachuted over a presidential monument."

In this instance, four Golden Knights left the aircraft at 2,500 feet as it passed over the banks of the Potomac. Eckbold was the first to land his black and gold canopy on the lush green lawn behind the Lincoln Memorial. He was followed by **Staff Sergeants John Luke** and **Dave Haberkorn** and **Sergeant Ken "K.C." Kassens**—the team's freefall photographer, respectively.

Haberkorn flew in the American flag, which waved in the breeze from his suspension lines as he passed over the Memorial, as a crowd of over 10,000 experienced a surge of patriotism. Millions of other Americans watched the jump via satellite.

"Viewing from the ground," said **Sergeant Cathleen Sherritt**, who was serving as ground control, "it went off perfectly. Everybody was right on time."

Sergeant Dan Molesky, who assisted Sherritt with ground control for this special jump in which timing had to be perfect, pointed out that the Knights actually brought the ceremonies back on schedule "with 14 seconds to spare." The Navy band coordinated with the Knights by playing the National Anthem at the moment the last jumper landed.

"Our jump was sandwiched between the introduction of the president and the playing of the National Anthem," said **Lieutenant Colonel Kirk Knight**, commander of the team. "The whole ceremony was contingent on our timing. But our aviation section did an excellent job putting the jumpers out over the right spot at the precise second, and the jumpers themselves did a superb job landing on target."

Chief Warrant Officers Four Mike Gornick and **Pete D'Agostino** who piloted that show and **Crew Chief Specialist Steve Leibach** had other factors to consider than just the timing. Most of Washington, D.C. is restricted air space, and though the FAA (Federal Aeronautics Association) had allowed the team a waiver to fly over the Memorial, the flight path they were given was itself extremely restrictive.

The inauguration committee was confident in the abilities of the Army Parachute Team to be on time and on target.

A model of the C-47 (DC-3) used by the team for a number of years. It was a C-47 that crashed at Silk Hope, N.C. in 1973, killing all 14 members of the Army Parachute Team aboard.

But just in case there were any questions in the minds of members of Congress who tend to question everything in which the U.S. military is involved, their doubts were put to rest by news anchorman Charlie Gaddy of WRAL-TV5 of Raleigh, North Carolina, who was on hand and live for the ceremonies.

"They're simply the best," Gaddy said of the Golden Knights. "That's why they're here."

Later that same summer, "the best" would find the target itself was in restrictive space, but as another former Black Team leader, **Master Sergeant** (retired) **Fred Patterson** explains it, the most difficult jumps are preferred by the Black Team. In a performance at Ocean City, Maryland, their target was a 40-ft. by 80-ft. floating platform that looked like a matchbox on the river from jump altitude (12,500 feet). The team's X-shaped target stood out like a tiny orange spot on the surface of the water. Nonetheless, each member of the

Black Team found the target and avoided a splash entry into the show.

Staff Sergeant Doug Lane led off the show as flag jumper and narrator. He was followed by **Staff Sergeant John Luke** and **Sergeant Harvey Wainer** doing the Baton Pass. **Sergeant Jeff Kimbrell** stole the show momentarily with the Cutaway maneuver until **Sergeants K.C. Kassens** and **Bill Godwin** streaked across the sky in the Diamond Track maneuver. The team's executive officer, **Captain Marcus Bonds**, joined **Sergeant First Class Paul Guerra, Staff Sergeant Dave Haberkorn** and **Specialist Phil Peyton** in the Diamond formation. Ground Control for that particular jump— **Sergeant Gary Salmans**, found himself more than a little busy snatching canopies from the clutches of the wind after each jumper landed on target, to prevent them from going into the water, as the length of their suspension lines would have allowed the chutes to hang over the side of the unusually small target platform.

Following the show, the Black Team members were brought to shore by boat and introduced to the crowd in a lineup formation. Afterwards, each man moved off into the grass to pack his parachute and answer questions from the hundreds of spectators who followed admiringly. They wanted to know more about the team and the Army, and get autographs from

these top-notch young men who formed the Knights' Black Demonstration Team.

The Black Team has performed in more than a few difficult jumps. They were the first to jump near Mount Rushmore; into a baseball stadium; and the first to perform Canopy Relative Work during an air show. Team members themselves have other favorites among the shows they've performed. According to **Staff Sergeant Mason Gallagher**—Black Team member from 1982 to 1985, the bigger air

shows like those in Chicago and Dayton were always his favorites. And yet, like every Knight, he has many special memories from smaller shows.

"The big shows had huge crowds and the sheer numbers of people made those shows unforgettable," he explained. "But the little shows—the ones we did into small town high school stadiums, those are the ones that stand out. You don't remember the name of the town, but you remember the people...the kids especially. They made those shows special."

Loy B. Brydon, U.S. Team member—1958-'59-'60-'61-'62-'63 and 1964, has made more dead-center landings than any man in the world. He also has made more freefalls than any man in the United States. Brydon also designed all parachute gear used by U.S. Teams since 1959.

Just as certain shows stand out in the memories of Golden Knights, certain members of the Black Demonstration Team stand out as well. Past and present members of the team are all different and yet all the same. Two former and two current Black Team members reveal their individuality and overall similarities: Staff Sergeant Tom Shriver, Master Sergeant (retired) Fred Patterson, Sergeant K.C. Kassens and Sergeant First Class Paul Guerra. They are typical of the members of this special group.

STAFF SERGEANT TOM SHRIVER

Army SSgt. William "Tom" Shriver, a Fairland, Indiana native, is a photographer who makes his backdrops wherever he finds them, and he usually finds them at 12,000 feet.

He prefers a basic backdrop of sky blue unless the weather is hazy; in which case, he adjusts his body position and camera angle to get a landscape backdrop. Shriver is a free-fall photographer and former member of the Black Demonstration Team.

"Ever since I can remember, I've loved photography," he said. "When I was 10, I entered a 4-H Club photo contest. I didn't win anything, but I think it's ironic that I entered a photo essay of myself dressed up as a soldier."

Shriver continued to develop his camera skills through practice and reading every available book on photography. A few months before he was to graduate from Triton Central High School, his art teacher suggested he talk to an Air Force recruiter about being a military photographer.

"I went down to the recruiting office," he explained. "The Air Force guy was out to lunch, but this other guy said he could help me. I figured, 'What the heck? They all wear green.' It didn't matter to me whether it was Air Force or Army, so long as I

Staff Sergeant Tom Shriver

was a photographer."

Shriver enlisted in the Army immediately following his high school graduation in June 1977. He graduated as the Distinguished Honor Graduate from his initial training photography school and was assigned as the personal photographer to Major General George S. Patton, Jr. at Stuttgart, West Germany.

In 1982 he was serving as a forensic photographer assigned to Fort Ord, Calif. and preparing to leave the Army.

"I was doing some freelance work for a civilian newspaper," he said. "The editor wanted me to cover, and I quote, 'Some guys who jump out of airplanes.'"

The guys he photographed were the Golden Knights. Shriver was particularly taken with the equipment worn by the team's freefall photographer. He reenlisted the following Monday and was at Fort Benning, Georgia attending airborne school a week later.

After jump school, Shriver came to Fort Bragg, North Carolina to serve as a reconnaissance photographer for 7th Special Forces. While in this assignment, he began skydiving and preparing himself to tryout for the Golden Knights.

In 1986, Shriver succeeded during the Knights' annual tryout program. He was selected as a demonstrator on the Knights' Black Demonstration Team where he soon began jumping a 35mm still and 8mm video camera mounted on a lightweight helmet.

"My most memorable air show was the opening ceremonies of the 1987 Pan-American Games held in my hometown," he said. "I think my favorite photo I took while a Golden Knight, was the opening ceremonies of Bush's presidential inauguration."

In addition to being a parachute demonstrator and freefall photographer for the Knights, Shriver earned the title, "Voice of the Golden Knights" serving as a team narrator.

His photography and speaking skills led to his ultimately moving from a position as a fulltime demonstrator, to being a photographer and press coordinator in the team's media relations office.

As senior photographer and supervisor of the team's photo lab, Shriver says he was able to ensure only quality photos of the Knights' two demonstration and two competition teams were released for publication, or presented as special matted photos.

"My dream, or let's say 'goal,' in life is to some day own my own portrait studio," Shriver said.

He says he also dreams of joining an aerobatic flying team. That adventurous side of him is revealed in some of the hobbies he enjoys, including scuba diving, golf, and participating in the grueling run, swim and cycling competition called the triathlon.

But all his hobbies, including skydiving, remain seconded by his one true love—photography.

MASTER SERGEANT (RETIRED) FRED PATTERSON

Private Fred Patterson III was pretty much at ease as he sat in the first sergeant's office—a place most young soldiers prefer to avoid. But he was even leaning back in the "old man's" chair and seemed to be contemplating whether to prop his feet on his desk. The old man, after all, was his father, Master Sergeant Fred Patterson, Jr., and he probably wouldn't...on second thought, he probably would mind. He sat upright, almost at attention.

The younger Patterson came into the Army because there wasn't anything exciting to do at home in Dandridge, Tennessee. His father's decision to come in the Army was far less complicated. He was drafted in 1968.

"Dandridge is the second oldest town in Tennessee," Patterson said, explaining his son's decision to follow him in the Army. "To this day,

it still doesn't have a stop light. There's not a lot to do there but hunt and fish, which is fine with me. I was 24 when I got my draft notice. I guess you could say I was 'country as an outside toilet'—stayed in the woods most of the time."

Patterson retired shortly after his son joined the Army and returned to the woods to catch up on missed hunting seasons. He had over 20 years service, more than six years of which were with the Army Parachute Team. With over 4,000 parachute jumps and "a fishing story" for each jump, it's little wonder his son followed him into the airborne. Whether he will ever wear the black and gold uniform his father wore so proudly, his father says only time will tell. The younger Patterson was about to enrole in a freefall class that day in his father's office. Patterson was custodian of the 82d Sport Parachute Club until he retired in August 1989. He preferred introducing his son to the sport through

Master Sergeant (retired) Fred Patterson, former Black Demonstration Team leader and team first sergeant.

the "old" freefall classes rather than AFF (Accelerated Freefall). His son now has a "Class B" license.

"The only thing wrong with accelerated freefall is you start out and a year later you can only have your D license and 200 jumps," he explained. "A whole bunch of jumps don't make you a good jumper. Until you've had some longevity in the sport—I mean, you learn things sitting around the clubs watching a rigger pack a parachute the right way. Just putting lines in a log book doesn't make you a good or safe jumper. And a lot of young jumpers get hurt 'cause they started out too quickly.''

The senior Patterson started skydiving while he was stationed at Fort Benning, Georgia assigned to the 75th Ranger Battalion and the 197th Infantry Brigade. He joined a local parachute club and started jumping— not a lot, but enough, he said. He was reassigned to Korea in 1970 and was assigned to the 82d Airborne Division at Fort Bragg, North Carolina on his return to the states.

''That's when I met **'Spider' Wrenn**,'' Patterson said. ''He was custodian of the 82d Club then. Man, he made us have a full field layout inspection-type thing before every demo...personally inspected our uniforms every day. The year I went to tryouts in '76, nine of the 11 guys selected were from the 82d Club. Spider was

the one who got me to put in my application. I wasn't sure I was ready.''

Just after Patterson was assigned to the team, Wrenn, who had served on the team 1966-69, became the team first sergeant. With Wrenn running the show, Patterson knew his first year was going to be both challenging and rewarding.

Patterson was assigned to the Black Demonstration Team and notes one of the first things he did was an historic jump at Mount Rushmore. A friendly rivalry between the Black and Gold teams was the incentive for doing the jump. Earlier, Gold Team members had flown over the site and decided it was a jump that couldn't be done. The Black Team, Patterson related, refused to be told any jump was impossible. Not only did they do the jump, silhouetting their black and gold canopies against the snow-covered monument, two of them carried a huge

banner in freefall that read: EAT YOUR HEART OUT, GOLD TEAM! Of course, says Patterson, they got photographs of the jump and, to add injury to insult, they photographed the banner, too!

After two years as a member of the Black Team, Patterson became team leader. He notes a jump into Philadelphia's Veteran's Stadium among one of his many accomplishments as team leader.

''To the best of my knowledge, no military team had ever jumped into a stadium,'' he admitted. ''And Veteran's Stadium is kind of unique in that you can sit anywhere in the stadium and not get wet if it rains. It's kind of a cone. We placed jumpers on 1st, 2nd and 3rd (base) then left field and right field and finally on the pitcher's mound.''

He says his team was also the first to do CRW (canopy relative work) during a demonstration. Their doing so caught both the spectators and his chain of command by surprise, he said, laughing. Until they did it, no one in the airshow business knew anything about CRW. And because the crowds loved it, it was incorporated into the regular show. Of course, he first had to explain the why's and how's of the maneuver "two feet front and centered" before the commander's desk.

Patterson left the team in 1981 and ran the 82d Club for a year before being assigned to a mechanized infantry unit in Germany. On his return to Fort Bragg, Patterson began running the Green Beret Club until the job for first sergeant of the Golden Knights came open.

"You know, it's funny," he laughed. "I can remember a special spot in the 82d Club beside Spider's trophy case that was understood to be reserved for Golden Knights. If you were Joe Jumper just starting out, you kind of walked around them...like they glowed or something. You were not in the same league as those guys...never."

But Patterson was in the Golden Knight league—twice. Having spent four years with the team as a demonstrator, he returned to the team as first sergeant for nearly three more years. While first sergeant, he squeezed in a few more memorable jumps, his favorite being a jump at the Pro Bowl in Hawaii and a nationwide tour of Australia.

Patterson says he looks back on his military career as an education in memories. That day in his office at the 82d Club, he offered his son some advice as he started his own airborne memories with a "war story" (as opposed to a fishing story this time) he thought was relevant. Old soldiers know a lot of "war stories," and if one of those old soldiers happens to be your father, you're likely to hear a lot of them—some, several times! But if you want to learn, you'll listen. Young Patterson seemed to be listening just fine!

Sergeant Ken Kassens, former Black Demonstration Team member and freefall photographer.

SERGEANT K.C. KASSENS

By the time Sergeant Ken "K.C." Kassens graduated from Cedarburg High School near Milwaukee, Wisconsin in 1982, he had lettered three years as a member of his school's diving team. Today, he still enjoys water sports and he still enjoys "diving." His jump platform, however, is considerably higher than it used to be and he no longer lands in water!

And if monogram letters were given, Kassens would have earned several by now for having served more than four years with the Golden Knights' Black Demonstration Team. During those years, he jumped in 43 of our 50 states, as well as Canada. As much as he loves "skydiving," however, he says he's just proud to be a soldier.

"I went through my entire senior year of high school knowing what I was going to do when I graduated," he boasted. "My friends were trying to figure out what they were going to do, but I knew I was going to be a soldier."

Kassens had enlisted as delayed-entry at the start of his senior year. Two weeks after graduation, he was off to basic training where he would ultimately be trained as an airborne, single-channel radio operator. In February 1983, he was assigned to the 82d Airborne Division at Fort Bragg, North Carolina. Almost immediately upon his arrival, he began sky-

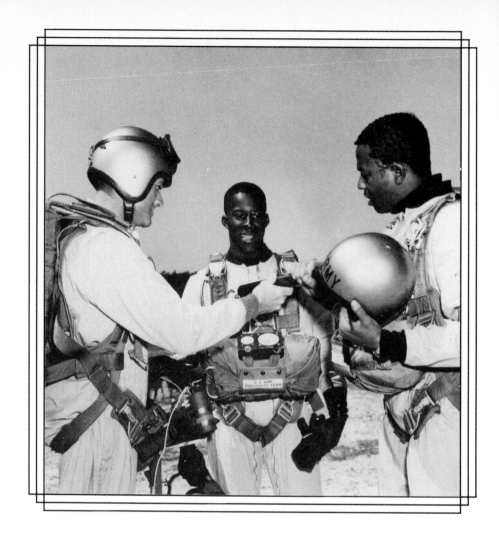

diving by joining the XVIII Airborne Corps Sport Parachute Club.

"I originally joined the Army with the intent of doing a couple of years, getting out and going to college," he admitted. "But once I got in and started jumping, I decided I liked the Army and reenlisted."

Kassens was selected to the team following Tryouts in 1985. His

specific duties included being a flag jumper and narrator. He also served as a freefall photographer. In fact, he says approximately 650 of his nearly 2,600 freefall parachute jumps were with a still and video camera mounted on his helmet.

Of the thousands of shows in which he performed, Kassens, like all members of the Army

Parachute Team, has his favorites. Topping the list, was the parachute exhibition the Black Team did for then President-elect George Bush at the inauguration ceremonies. His air-to-air video of that jump was provided to a television network and aired nationwide, which, he admits, is one more reason he'll treasure that particular show.

Other shows he considers his favorites include the Appalachian Fair in Johnson City, Tennessee, the Pro Bowl in Honolulu, Hawaii and one he did for the hometown folks in the 1986 City of Festivals Parade in Milwaukee. This show was really special for obvious reasons as he recalls with a big grin how he landed before the crowds gathered at the intersection of N. 4th St. and W. Kilbourne.

"I like to travel and I like the Army way of life," he said, summing up his reasons for remaining a soldier.

It was during his travels as a Golden Knight that Kassens met his wife, Angela, who's originally from London.

"We met at a show in Tulsa, Oklahoma," he explained. "She was visiting a relative there who just happened to be part of the air show committee. We stayed in touch, and...well, we got married in July 1988."

He and Angela began traveling together in March 1990, as Kassens left the Golden Knights for Germany and his first overseas assignment. He says he was just as excited about going to Europe as she was about returning. Their tour in Germany will be a minimum of four years. He smiles broadly when asked about his future. "The Army," he'll answer, "is my future."

Sergeant First Class Paul Guerra, current Black Demonstration Team leader.

SERGEANT FIRST CLASS PAUL GUERRA

He prefers the toughest assignments, those that present a continuous learning challenge. That's why Sergeant First Class Paul Guerra chose to become a Ranger, a HALO (high altitude, low opening) jump instructor and a Golden Knight. After his first year on the Army Parachute Team in 1989, Guerra's earnest desire for greater challenges

143

and responsibilities led to his becoming team leader of the Black Demonstration Team.

Ranger units, as part of the Rapid Deployment Force, are used extensively in special missions behind enemy lines, such as raids or rescue missions like the 1983 rescue of American students in Grenada. Guerra was with the 2nd Battalion 75th Rangers when they rescued those American students. HALO-qualified soldiers are able to deploy behind enemy lines quickly without being detected by the enemy. Guerra trained soldiers to be HALO qualified. The Golden Knights, of course, are also a one-of-a-kind unit as the Army's only official aerial demonstration unit. And Guerra, like all Golden Knights, is a one-of-a-kind soldier.

"If there's no challenge, it's not worth doing," Guerra said, explaining his philosophy of life. "You've got to keep learning something new because when you think you know it all

and stop learning, you're not serving any function. You've got nothing to do."

As a senior NCO with 11 years in the Army, Guerra says with a grin that he ensures the troops under his supervision always have "something to do." But he leads by example, always volunteering for the toughest schools and assignments the Army has to offer.

He began running his self-imposed education gauntlet after graduating high school in Silver City, New Mexico in 1979. He enlisted as a

radio operator with the 2nd Ranger Battalion at Fort Lewis, Washington, but later changed his MOS (military occupational specialty) after completing Ranger School in 1980. Four years later, he was reassigned to the 75th Ranger Regiment at Fort Benning, Georgia. Enroute to Benning, he attended the three-week long HALO School. Guerra did so well during the course, the school cadre offered him a job.

"When I graduated from HALO School, I was offered a job as an instructor," he explained. "I felt I needed more experience skydiving though, but I soon got that because parachuting soon became my only interest."

Setting his mind to improving his jumping skills, Guerra accepted an instructor's position with the HALO Committee at Fort Bragg, North Carolina about a year later. His primary courses of instruction included body stabilization and emergency procedures. His work day usually began around 2 a.m. and ran well into the evening. Now that he's a demonstrator/team leader with the Golden Knights, he travels with the Black Team every weekend from early March to late November. He and his team also spend 4-6 weeks winter training in Yuma, Arizona each Jan.-Feb., which altogether keeps him away from home up to 280 days a year.

"I sometimes miss working with students," Guerra admitted. "But I think it's a challenge of a different type to work with the public as I do now."

Guerra says his wife, Tina, and their two daughters support his constant pursuit of tougher and tougher assignments. A normal tour with the Golden Knights is three years. When he completes his tenure, Guerra already plans to return to another Ranger unit or volunteer for Special Forces. He emphasizes that the Army has plenty of challenges left for him. At the moment, however, he intends to take every opportunity to represent the Army in a positive way as a Golden Knight.

THE GOLD DEMONSTRATION TEAM

All it took was two or three people on the ground pointing skyward and 75,000 football fans diverted their attention from the marching band to a black and gold airplane passing over the stadium.

"They're gonna jump!" a man shouted above a crowd momentarily hushed.

True to his prediction, nine dark figures emerged from the cargo doors of an F27 Fokker, then flashed black and gold canopies over Sun Devil Stadium in Phoenix, Arizona. They were members of the Golden Knights' Gold Demonstration Team.

The occasion for their dropping in was the 18th Annual Fiesta Bowl—the battle for first place in NCAA college football. It wasn't the first time the Golden Knights had jumped at the Fiesta Bowl, and judging from the enthusiastic reaction of the Fighting Irish and Mountaineer fans, it wouldn't be the last.

"It was about as near to being a perfect jump as anybody could hope for," said **Sergeant First Class Ben Currin**, team leader of the Gold Team. "Everybody was right on time and right on target."

Currin explained that every stadium jump required special precautions, as well as a practice jump, which his team did the day before. The practice jump uncovered both known and unexpected problems. Any stadium jump presents hazards such as wires, light poles and changing winds, but Sun Devil Stadium is directly in line with the runway of Sky Harbor Airport. With these points in mind, the actual parachute exhibition was pegged between the Notre Dame Marching Band and the National Anthem. As the band began their final number, the Knights left the plane at 4,000 feet and opened their chutes at 2,500 feet.

Golden Knight pilots—**Captain James Daley** and **Chief Warrant Officer Four Mike Gornick**, and **Crew Chief Specialist Todd Morton**, maintained communications with the ground control **Sergeant First Class Mike Mayo** and **Sergeant Chuck Roberts** and the airport, while dodging commercial airlines which seemed to be constantly crossing their flight path.

As the jumpers entered the stadium from north to south, they were surprised to see themselves on a giant video screen. Not only did they have a captive audience within the stadium, their aerial demonstration was carried live via satellite!

'"That's me!' I told myself," Currin said as he saw his own landing approach on television. "It was the best feeling you can imagine."

Currin and **Sergeant Craig Girard**, a Phoenix native, were the first to land. They were followed by a series of flag jumpers. **Sergeants Jeff Steele** and **Kevin Peyton** flew in the West Virginia and Indiana (Notre Dame) state flags, respectively. **Staff Sergeant Nick Nichols** jumped in the official Fiesta Bowl flag while **Staff Sergeant John Luke**, who was visiting from the Knights' Black Demonstration Team for this special show, flew in the NBC flag.

A 2-stack formation consisting of **Staff Sergeant Ed Rivera** and **Sergeant John Steele** brought in the American flag. **Sergeant Jake Brown**—the team freefall photographer, was the last Knight to hit the Fiesta Bowl logo centered on the 50-yardline and hurry off the field amid screams from a crowd which was only quieted by the playing of the National Anthem.

Arizona is a beautiful state from the ground, or at jump altitude. Rocky mountain peaks surround Sun Devil Stadium, along with huge cactus plants that look like human silhouettes, all of which made the Fiesta Bowl jump particularly spectacular for the jumpers and the fans. But it is cold in Arizona in January. Five months later, the Gold Team would make nine much warmer jumps at Cypress Gardens, Florida, during the Memorial Day weekend—also a beautiful place to jump.

At 5,000-feet, Central Florida is noticeably flat and covered with snow-white sand amid various shades of green—from olive-green lawns and fields, to dark-green orange groves. Hundreds of smoke-colored

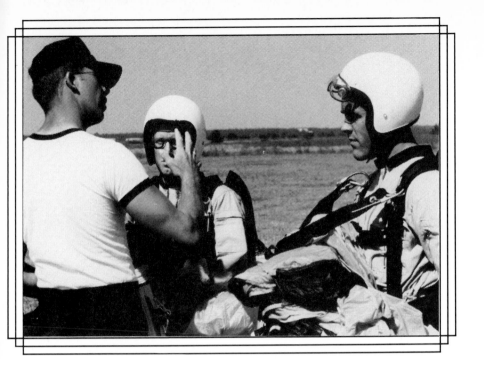

ponds and lakes dot the countryside, many surrounded by moss-covered cypress trees and an occasional palm. Rows of ranch-style homes align themselves along blacktop roadways, each home with its own sparkling blue swimming pool.

At 5,000-feet, the ground temperature—which stays in the upper 90's from late May until mid-September, has been cooled four degrees for every 1000-feet of altitude.

And yet, as the F27 Fokker continues to gain altitude, Gold Team members joke with each other, seemingly oblivious to the open cargo doors near the rear of the plane and the chilling winds coming through them.

It's 11:30 a.m. and the elite aerial demonstration team is preparing to make yet another jump into Cypress Gardens' family-oriented theme park as part of a Memorial Day "Salute to the Military."

The team's pilots, **Chief Warrant Officers Four Pete D'Agostino** and **Doug Creef**, receive a message from the Ground Control, **Staff Sergeant Mark French**,

two miles below. The crew chief, **Private First Class Larry Denning**, relays the message to the assistant team leader, **Staff Sergeant Ed Rivera**, who in turn passes the message on to **Ben Currin**.

A hand signal is used to relay the message, hands crossed at the wrists forming an X. To these men, the signal means they have a hot target below. In little more than a minute, **Sergeant Chuck Roberts**, today's flag jumper and narrator, approaches the left cargo door.

He turns and faces the front of the plane, then exits the aircraft by stepping out sideways, arms and legs stretched and arched. For this particular jump, Roberts carries a section of today's newspaper, explaining that he hadn't had time to read about yesterday's three jumps and figures he'll catch up on his reading while in freefall.

Seconds tick by as his teammates gather at both cargo doors in preparation to join him, including **Currin** and

Rivera and **Staff Sergeants Nick Nichols, Jason Davis** and **Hank Turner** along with **Sergeants Jeff and John Steele** (no relation), **Jake Brown** and **Eric Folkestad**. At the count of three, all nine remaining Knights exit the aircraft in mass to add to the already spectacular entertainment provided at Cypress Gardens.

"It's one of our favorite shows," Currin explained. "They treat us like honored guests here, and we really appreciate that."

Being treated like "honored guests" isn't a prerequisite to choosing what shows the Gold Team will do. Himself a former Army recruiter, Currin knows the value of generating and maintaining good public relations. Gold Team members, like their teammates on the Black Team, appreciate a challenge. The kind of challenge they appreciate most is getting through to crowds of spectators seemingly disinterested in the what the Army Parachute

Team is all about and what they do. They achieve this goal with a squad of gregarious personalities, men like former team members **Staff Sergeant Nick Nichols** and **Master Sergeant Mark Shields**, and current team members **Rivera** and **Currin**.

STAFF SERGEANT NICK NICHOLS

While attending Lincoln Sudbury High School in Boston, Massachusetts, Staff Sergeant Richard "Nick" Nichols proved himself to be gifted in the acrobatic skills necessary to perform on the high bar, parallel bars and rings. He was so gifted, in fact, Nick was responsible for forming his school's first gymnastic team during his senior year in 1971.

About 14 years after graduating from high school, Nichols proved himself gifted in the aerobatic skills necessary for the sport of parachuting. He was selected as a member of

Staff Sergeant Richard "Nick" Nichols, former Gold Demonstration Team member.

the Golden Knights' Gold Demonstration Team. Originally a Special Forces medic, Nichols was selected to the Knights after team Tryouts in 1985.

"Before I joined the Army, I'd never even flown in a plane," he explained. "Three years after I joined, I went to Airborne School at Fort Benning (Georgia), and two years later while I was stationed with a Special Forces group in Germany, I started skydiving."

Nichols was attending

Dean Junior College in Boston when he decided to join the Army in September 1973. During two back-to-back tours in Germany, he met his wife, Katrina, and he traveled with the Special Forces (Europe) Parachute Team, performing in aerial demonstrations and competing in parachute competitions.

"I was also an instructor for one of those 'outward bound' type things where high school students get to go out in the woods and be taught things like orienteering and survival techniques," he said. "I enjoyed doing that."

In 1985 Nichols was returning from a break in service to an assignment as an airborne medic with the 82d Airborne Division at Fort Bragg, North Carolina.

"I wanted to improve my skydiving skills," he explained. "So, I submitted an application to try out for the Golden Knights."

Nichols only had 350 freefall parachute jumps when he came to Tryouts. He didn't really ex-

pect to make the team, but was hoping to benefit from the training enough to be selected the following year. He shouldn't have been so surprised to have been selected, though. After all, aerobatics are not so terribly different from acrobatics. Both sports involve body control, timing and determination. A big plus was his outstanding soldierly attitude, his motivation, and peer leadership during Tryouts.

When he left the team in November 1989 for yet another tour in Germany, he had over 1,500 jumps to his credit. Among his additional duties to being a parachute demonstrator, Nichols was a presentation team leader—a job in which he supervised three other NCO's in public appearances such as high school or college presentations, or during hospital visits. Nichols says he particularly enjoyed talking with kids, not only about the team and the Army, but the importance of staying in school and staying away from drugs

and alcohol.

"I'd say about 90 percent of a Golden Knight's job is public relations...you know, talking to kids and adults. To me, it's the best part of the job," Nichols said seriously. "But I also liked sharing the same sport with my teammates, who shared the same ideals about the military and took pride in promoting the Army."

Nichols says his most memorable moment on the Army Parachute Team was being part of the 1989 military record 45-way formation over Yuma, Arizona. During that jump, 45 Golden Knights linked together hand-in-hand in freefall to form the largest all-military "star" formation on record. The previous record was also set by the Golden Knights back in 1983. Plans are already in the making to break the '89 record in 1990 by forming a 60-way formation. Nichols admits he'd like to be part of that record attempt, as well.

"We completed our formation on our first

try," he boasted. "Then we held it together for 22 seconds before we had to break off. It was great to be a part of that."

Although the record jump was unforgettable, Nichols took more than a little pride during an air show at Hanscom Air Force Base near Boston in 1989. During this show—one of his last as a member of the Golden Knights, Nichols was able to show friends and family how he turned the acrobatic skills he impressed them with in high school and won gymnastic competitions, into aerobatic skills which won the admiration of his peers and fellow countrymen.

Master Sergeant Mark Shields, former Gold Demonstration Team leader.

MASTER SERGEANT MARK SHIELDS

While he was trying to enlist in the Air Force in 1970, Mark Shields received a letter from the Army inviting him to come to work—only it wasn't actually an invitation. He was being drafted. Since he was planning on joining the service anyway, Shields decided to get one jump ahead of the Army and have some choice about the job he'd be doing. He enlisted as a radio operator with an air-

borne option—an option he cashed in on. By the start of the following year, he was assigned to 82d Signal Corp at Fort Bragg, and looking for a way to get in a few more jumps.

"I had started a static line freefall course back home," he said. "But the weather turned bad and I only made one jump before the Army called me to make a quick decision. The next time I jumped was in Airborne School."

In July 1971, Shields again picked up his schooling to become a parachutist by joining the 82d Sport Parachute Club. The club custodian—Spider Wrenn, had just returned from Vietnam and had broken his leg on his first jump since leaving for Vietnam.

"Spider was one of my instructors," Shields said, grinning. "When I met him, he was in a cast, but he didn't let it slow him down. We formed the first 82d Demo Team that year, did jumps in front of Iron Mike. We had red, white and blue (All

Shields "spotting" for a demonstration jump.

American Division colors) canopies."

The demonstration experience helped out a lot when he tried out for the Golden Knights in 1972, but he was dropped for administrative reasons just the same. Following the March 1973 crash, Shields was called back to the team in May. He "pulled" ground control for the Black Team for a few weeks until his first sergeant was satisfied he was up to performing in demonstrations, then Shields went to the Gold Team. In August, the Department of Defense closed down the team, along with the Thunderbirds and Blue Angels while they decided whether the teams should be disbanded in the face of the fuel crisis.

"**Captain Needles** made a trip up to Washington, D.C. to defend the team," Mark said. "We were only down a week or so, had to cancel a couple midseason shows, but not many, I don't think."

When the fuel crisis was settled, Shields traveled with a composite team to Brazil in September for an international airshow. Notwithstanding the memories of the show itself, he mostly recalls his bus drivers—Heckle and Jeckle, so-named by the team—whom he says only knew two things about driving: press the accelerator to the floor and lean on the horn as you fly around mountain passes on two wheels!

Shields left the team in 1977, only to return in '79 by going through tryouts again. Except, he really didn't go through tryouts because he spent most of his time training with the Relative Work Team. Throughout the next year, he was a freefall photographer for the relative work team.

"I video-taped the 8-way competition at the nationals in 1980," he said. "They were going to use it to judge the competition, but it never did pan-out. They weren't ready for air-to-air video."

Eight years later, air-to-air video would become an integral part of relative work competition at the nationals.

Shields returned to the

Gold Team following the nationals that year. During the 1982 and 1983 show season, he was team leader, leading his team to jumps such as the Pro Bowl in Hawaii and Super Bowl XVII.

"We had to be 50-feet up when they came back from a commercial, no excuses," he explained. "I had to stand on the ground and count the seconds to get the timing down perfect. But it went perfectly, and we got 56 seconds of worldwide coverage."

The following year was a busy one for Shields. He began it by leading the Gold Team in a victory jump into Grenada. After that jump, he left the team for 17 weeks to attend the Advanced NCO Course. On his return, he was part of the tryout cadre and he personally coordinated everything for the team's 1984 Reunion. In between tryouts and the reunion, he got married.

"I met Linda on the road," he explained. "She was doing public relations for an airshow. I thought she was a

news reporter or something, so I was leading her all around the plane, introducing her to the team. Anyway, when we got married, I was running the reunion, so we didn't have time for a honeymoon."

From January to June 1985, Shields worked in the team's operations office pending his reassignment to Germany. The desk time, he said, allowed him some much needed time to spend with his bride. Today, Shields is a master sergeant assigned to the 82d Airborne Division, still very active in parachuting.

Staff Sergeant Ed Rivera, current Gold Demonstration assistant team leader.

STAFF SERGEANT ED RIVERA

There wasn't a drop zone within 200 miles of his hometown of Silver City, New Mexico, no parachutists falling out of the sky to inspire him. And yet, Staff Sergeant Ed Rivera, now the assistant team leader of the Golden Knights' Gold Demonstration Team and one of two Silver City natives on the Golden Knights, lived with a burning desire to jump out of airplanes.

"My uncle was airborne, and my brother was a parachute rigger," Rivera explained. "They told me enough stories about jumping to get me interested in doing it myself. Besides, military service is a family tradition. My father is a Korean War veteran, and just about every male member of my family has served in one branch of the service or another."

Despite his desire to "go airborne," however, Rivera joined a local labor union following his graduation from Cobre High School in 1972. The union promptly sent him off to school where he learned to cut, weld, lay pipe and concrete and a number of other highly skilled laborman's jobs.

He became an industrial mechanic working with various underground equipment such as diamond drills and rock crushers used in mining operations. When his union went on strike with the copper mining company he was

SSG Ed Rivera, Assistant Gold Demonstration Team leader, is escorted from the drop zone (the team's own backyard) by his son, Joshua, after he and his teammates returned from winter training in Yuma, Arizona, February 26, 1990. Once he was off the drop zone, Joshua helped his father pack his parachute, hurrying him to come on home after his five-week absence. Unknown to him, his father packed his chute as many as eight times a day, every day during winter training.

working for in 1978, Rivera decided it was time to make a move and join the Army.

"I wanted to do something for myself and my country," Rivera said. "I enlisted to be an airborne armor crewman after my recruiter convinced me how great it would be to 'drive, load, gun, shoot, move and communicate with 54 tons of cold, metabolic steel.'"

He grinned mischieviously as he mimicked his recruiter—dark Indian eyes gleaming and chuckling to himself. Rivera's initial assignment was as a Sheridan crewman supporting the 82d Airborne Division at Fort Bragg, North Carolina. After graduating from jump school, Rivera was assigned to Fort Bragg in September of 1978. Jumping was everything he thought it would be and more. In December of the same year, he began skydiving with the XVIII Airborne Corps Sport Parachute Club. At this time, he also observed his first Golden Knight

aerial demonstration and knew this would be his ultimate goal.

Rivera tried out for the team in 1981 and was selected. He says there was a mix-up in his stabilization and he received orders for Germany within a year after coming to the team. He and his wife, Anna, had been married only a few weeks when they left Fort Bragg for Europe. His new assignment with the 1st Armored Division as a tank commander consisted mostly of monitoring the Czechoslovakian border.

Despite his armor mission, however, Rivera continued to hone his jumping skills, even earning his British parachutist wings through an exchange with a British airborne regiment. In 1985, Rivera again tried out for the Golden Knights and was again accepted to the team. As an assistant team leader, he is responsible for accountability of 12 teammates and for conducting most of the training and equipment maintenance.

Rivera is also responsible for his teammates' conduct, a job he says is no job at all.

"There's no discipline problems on this team," he explained. "There's a lot of camaraderie among team members. We're all enthusiastic about being here. Everybody has their own individual responsibilities to make the team work."

As a parachute demonstrator, Rivera is on the road, away from home up to 280 days a year. When he's not out training or performing away from home, he says he prefers the quiet time at home with his wife and their 3-year old son, Joshua. Without making any predictions, Rivera says he would not be surprised to see his son follow the Rivera family tradition and serve his country. For that matter, he added, he wouldn't be surprised if young Joshua grew up with a burning desire to jump out of airplanes!

Sergeant First Class Ben Currin, current Gold Demonstration Team leader.

SERGEANT FIRST CLASS BEN CURRIN

Sergeant First Class Ben Currin seizes every opportunity to promote the Army, both as a means of retaining and recruiting good soldiers, and for the chance to instill confidence in America's Army.

Currin, a native of Ox-ford, North Carolina, has made a career of promoting the Army, having served as a drill instructor, a recruiter and, today, team leader of the Golden Knights' Gold Demonstration Team.

He describes his current position as the capstone of his military career because he is now able to promote the Army—his "life since 18"—around the world, rather than a specific region of the country.

The son of Thomas and Lois Currin of Ox-ford, Ben Currin gradu-ated from John Nichols High School in 1968 and enlisted as an infantry-man. It was basic and advanced individual training at Fort Bragg, North Carolina and Fort Polk, Louisiana, respec-tively, then off to Viet-nam with the 101st Air-borne Division.

After a year in Viet-nam, Currin volunteered to be a drill instructor and spent the next four years training and pre-paring young troops for combat, making them into soldiers. In 1975, however, Ben elected to take a three year break from active duty, al-though he "stayed in touch" by serving in the active reserves. During half of that break, he at-tended North Carolina State University.

In 1978, Currin re-turned to active duty afresh and highly motivated, "coming off the street and going straight to jump school and the 82d Airborne Division." At jump school, Ben discovered he had a passion for jumping which couldn't be satisfied by an occa-sional static line training jump.

"I was just back from jump school and all about jumping," Currin said. "A friend of mine, Bill Friddle, got me to join the 82d Sport Para-chute Club just as he was getting ready to go through Golden Knights' Tryouts. Being in a parachute club, I could get three to four jumps a day."

At an air show in Dothan, Alabama in April 1988, Currin made his 2,000th freefall para-chute jump, proving his passion for jumping has yet to simmer despite a knee injury that nearly put him off jump status a few years ago.

Currin tried out for the Golden Knights in 1984 after serving successive tours as a recruiter in his hometown of Oxford, as well as Henderson, Roanoke Rapids and Greenville, North Carolina. He was accepted and assigned to the team in January 1985 as a parachute demonstrator.

"The mission of the Golden Knights," says Currin, "is to promote the U.S. Army through precision freefall parachuting." For Currin, however, his jumping days nearly ended in January 1986 during winter training in Yuma, Arizona. He tore several ligaments in his right knee while landing during a training jump.

"Sometimes we refer to torn ligaments as a sport parachutist's nightmare," he explained. "Unlike paratroopers in the 82d (Airborne Division) who tend to break bones from bad landings with heavy equipment, our worst injury is torn ligaments. Bones can usually be mended, but torn ligaments tend to stay torn."

Nonetheless, Currin never gave up hope of jumping again and elected for reconstructive surgery. Within nine months to the day of his injury, he was jumping again with his teammates, this time as assistant team leader. The 1990 show season began his sixth year as a Golden Knight, his third as the Gold Team leader.

"Since jumping is my job, each jump is important to me," he said. "What number of jump it is for me, or what show it is makes no difference. As far as safety is concerned, I treat each jump like it's my first. As far as performance is concerned, I strive for perfection."

Currin says he is grateful for every opportunity to talk with young people and anyone interested in the Golden Knights or the Army. Through his road trips, he has made friends around the country with various celebrities, including country singer Lee Greenwood and multi-millionaire H. Ross Perot.

More than anything else, Currin says he appreciates the support he receives at home from his wife, Nancy. He rarely gets a weekend at home, which he knows can be a burden for any wife and mother, especially his wife, who works full-time as a realtor in Fayetteville, North Carolina.

Despite the hardships placed on her by his long absences, Currin says Nancy fully supports him and is proud to be the wife of a Golden Knight. With her encouragement, Currin says promoting the Army and the Army way of life is not only his job, but his pleasure.

THE LOOPERS — THE STYLE & ACCURACY TEAM

The 1989 U.S. National Skydiving Championships ended July 13th, much to the relief of a lot of civilian competitors. The Army Parachute Team took seven of nine possible medals in the Style & Accuracy competition, to include the top three overall winners and first place in Style.

The 1988 Accuracy champion and Fort Bragg's Athlete of the Year—**Sergeant Chuck Lackey**, took first place overall. He was followed by teammates **Sergeant First Class Tom Welgos** and **Sergeant Kevin Breaux**, respectively.

Sergeant Bill Jackson grabbed the gold in Style with an average time of 7.02 seconds per round after four rounds. Welgos took the silver with 7.05 seconds per round. Lackey rounded out the Style competition for the Knights with fourth place.

Sergeant Randy Kern, the 1987 Accuracy champion, picked up the silver medal in the Accuracy competition with a total score of three centimeters after 10 rounds. Lackey took the bronze with four centimeters. The winning score of only two centimeters was set by civilian jumper, John Spears, who didn't compete in Style and therefore wasn't eligible for overall honors.

"It's probably the best we've done in Style & Accuracy in the past 10 years," said the Army team's coach, **Sergeant First Class Jim Nipper**, who's been a member of the team for nearly 10 years. "We've always picked up first in one event or the other, but, to my knowledge, we've never made such a clean sweep of the overall medals."

Nipper, who is himself a former national champion, served as a Style & Accuracy competitor for four years. This was his first year as team coach.

Sergeants First Class Brad Arvidson and **Gary Mohler** added to the Army's overall standings at the '89 Nationals by finishing 9th and 13th. Former Golden Knight **Gene Thacker** continued to compete in Style & Accuracy through his sons, **Tony** and **Tim**, who took fifth and seventh place overall.

According to Arvidson, Thacker not only coached his own sons to their current level of competitiveness, but was greatly responsible for training the current Golden Knight Style & Accuracy Team. Thacker, who is retired from the Army, traveled with the team to Yuma, Arizona during their 1988 Winter Training. "His coaching helped bring this particular Golden Knight Style & Accuracy Team to where it is today," said Arvidson.

And "where" is at the top! But then, Golden Knights have a reputation to maintain. There's nothing really unusual about a Golden Knight winning a gold medal, given the literal thousands of medals won by this team. Team members have walked away with medals and trophies from the U.S. Nationals every year since the team was conceived for that purpose by Joe Stilwell. There's nothing unusual about team members competing with each other, and in at least one case, brother against brother.

Brothers **Mark** and **Cliff Jones** battled for first place overall in Style & Accuracy at the 1983 and 1984 U.S. Nationals. News of their sibling rivalry even earned a special discussion by news commentator Paul Harvey. With the advent of additional female competitors, **Cheryl Stearns** even began to get some fierce competition by 1984 from her own teammates, **Terri Bennett Vares** and **Janice Captain**. "The intra-team rivalries have made the Knights more competitive internationally," explained Stearns. After all, if many of the best parachutists in the United States are Golden Knights, it would only be expected that their toughest competition would be from

among their own ranks.

Competition is the source of their motivation. Just as the demonstrators promote the Army through parachute demonstrations for many Americans, the competitors promote the Army through competitions from which they win the respect of their parachuting peers worldwide. As **Sergeant Kevin Breaux** aptly puts it, "The best way to get yourself noticed in the field of competition is to win. No one," says Breaux, "ever remembers who came in second."

The Loopers—a name given to them by teammates for their back-loops in the Style competition—discussed hereafter aren't second place, or second rate. Each one was, or is a national parachute champion. In addition to this aspect of the sport which draws men like **Sergeant Chuck Lackey, Master Sergeant Ray Duffy, Sergeant Bill Jackson** and **Staff Sergeant Jim Nipper** into the field of competition, there is each man's

desire to be his best and to test his ability against other competitors. Only then do they know if their training paid off!

Sergeant Chuck Lackey, current Style & Accuracy Team member, 1989 U.S. Nationals overall champion.

SERGEANT CHUCK LACKEY

When the smoke cleared after the 10th and final round of the Accuracy competition at the 1988 U.S. Nationals, a relative newcomer to parachute competition was the new National Accuracy champion. Sergeant Chuck Lackey took first place in a competition with 60 competitors, nearly all of whom had more competition experience than he did.

Later that summer, the national champ would compete in the World Parachute Championships in Nykoping, Sweden, and the World Cup Parachute Competition in Vichy, France. Then it was off to Seoul, South Korea, where he didn't have to compete in anything. Instead, Lackey jumped red, white and blue streamers from his suspension lines as he landed in the Olympic stadium as part of the opening ceremonies of the 1988 Summer Olympics.

"It was the proudest moment in my life," Lackey said, soft-spoken and sincere.

He says all he wanted to do when he joined the Army in 1982 was jump. But when he volunteered for Airborne School after being trained as a missile mechanic, he learned there were no airborne slots in that MOS (Military Occupational Specialty). But he didn't let that stop him from jumping. He took up skydiving during his off-duty hours.

By 1986, Lackey was so proficient in his after-duty hours hobby, he sent an application to the Golden Knights for Tryouts. His subsequent selection to the team caused a slight dilemma for his branch managers, he says, as one prerequisite to being a Golden Knight is being airborne qualified. There was nothing really unusual about Tryout selectees being sent away to Airborne School enroute to Fort Bragg and the Army Parachute Team. Lackey, however, not only needed Airborne School, he had to be retrained in another MOS—this time as a vulcan anti-aircraft gun mechanic, before he could be assigned to the Golden Knights. When he had completed his retraining, Lackey was assigned to the Knights' Gold Demonstration Team. But it became immediately apparent that his mind was set for competition.

"I'm a competitor at heart," he confessed. "Whatever I do, I like to do it better than anyone else."

After only one year as a demonstrator, Lackey tried out for the Style & Accuracy Team and proved himself capable of "turning loops" and hitting dead centers.

"I wasn't surprised at all," said **First Sergeant Jeff Moon** of Lackey's rapid advancement from demonstrator to competitor, from mere competitor to national champion. "I know how hard he's worked to get where he is. In the afternoon when the comp team finished practicing out at Raeford (North Carolina), I've seen Chuck pay for civilian lift tickets to make more practice jumps. When we were in Yuma for winter training, he would go jump with the demonstration teams when the comp teams quit for the day."

Moon describes Lackey as a man with

"an addiction" for jumping. Outside of his church and family life, Lackey admits his only interests are jumping and flying.

"Not too many people get to do their hobby for a living," he said, explaining that he concentrates all of his athletic ability on one sport—parachuting.

His high visibility victories in 1988 at the Nationals and at C.I.S.M. (Counseil Internationale du Sport Militare) in Brazil that same year led to his being selected as Fort Bragg's Male Athlete of the Year.

"I'd heard a rumor my name had been submitted for the award," Lackey shrugged, his Texas accent lingering in the air with quiet self-confidence. "But I didn't think I had much chance, having competed in only one sport and all."

During high school, Lackey says he played a variety of sports, including football, basketball, track and springboard diving. All these sports are very physical and highly competitive, but track and springboard diving were the two that probably helped him most in later years, he said.

"Whenever I'm with a group of people doing something, I refuse to be last," he explained. "As I said, I like to be competitive."

One of his teammates was responsible for introducing him to the sport in which he now excels, he explained. **Sergeant Randy Kern**, the 1987 National Accuracy champion, convinced Lackey to take up skydiving in 1983. Like Moon, Kern wasn't surprised when Lackey won a spot on the Style & Accuracy Team, although, with a grin, Kern admits he was a little surprised when the team rookie even beat him at the '88 Nationals. Lackey's subsequent victories at C.I.S.M. and his overall victory at the '89 Nationals only underscored his determination never to be last.

Whenever possible, Lackey has the fullest family support in parachute competitions.

His parents, Charles and Sharon Lackey always try to make it out to the Nationals to offer their moral support, as does his wife, Kenda, and their two children, Eric and Kristi. "Their support," he says, "makes those gold medals all the more worth striving for."

Despite his successes, Lackey "lacks" the large ego of someone at the very top of his field. When the Knights' Relative Work Team returned home to Fayetteville, North Carolina in October 1989 after successfully defending their world title in the 8-way Relative Work event, newspaper reporters and television news crews joined the entire team at the airport to greet them. One television reporter spotted Lackey standing in the team lineup awaiting his teammates' arrival and thought he'd get the gut feelings of a "typical" Golden Knight.

"So, tell me, Sir," he began, shoving a microphone in Lackey's face while a cameraman beamed in for a close-up shot of his nose. "You are a Golden Knight, are you not?"

"Yes, Sir," Lackey answered. "I'm Sergeant Chuck Lackey."

"Well, tell me something, Sergeant Lackey," the reporter insisted, looking from left to right as if the question he was about to ask was extremely confidential, "As you stand here waiting for your teammates who've just returned from Spain...I mean Spain!...and who're coming home world champions...world champions!...don't you...ah, don't you feel just a little bit envious?!"

"No Sir," Lackey answered without the slightest hesitation or hint of being insulted. "They're my teammates. Their victory is my victory, the whole team's victory. I'm extremely proud of them and how their win represents the United States and the U.S. Army. As far as my envying their competing in

an international competition, I competed in Sweden, France and Brazil last year and I'll compete in Yugoslavia next year. No Sir. We don't have to envy each other on this team."

He left the reporter somewhat speechless as he excused himself to re-join his teammates. When a representative from the Knights' media relations office pointed out that the Knight he had just interviewed was a two-time national champion, for a moment the reporter thought he understood why his line of questioning backfired.

"Well, no wonder," he said to the PAO. "So let me talk to a typical Golden Knight."

"Sergeant Lackey is a typical Golden Knight," he was told. "That's what makes the Golden Knights so special."

Master Sergeant (retired) Ray Duffy, former Style & Accuracy Team member, 1965 U.S. Nationals overall champion.

MASTER SERGEANT (RETIRED) RAY DUFFY

"What started as a sport for me turned out to be a fine and wonderful job with lifelong friends," explained Ray Duffy, president of the Golden Knight Alumni Association.

Duffy speaks fondly of two tours with the Golden Knights, his Yonkers, New York accent reverberating from the brick fireplace wall he was leaning against. Describing himself as a professional soldier, he came to the team in 1961 from the 101st Airborne Division at Fort Campbell, Kentucky.

"I came to the team right after the crash in '61—myself and Sherman Williford," he said, more slowly this time so that a Southerner could understand him. "A number of us came to the team then. That was because they had guys who were injured and needed people to take their places temporarily."

But Duffy said his first year was a little stormy due to seemingly endless attempts to shut down the team because of the crash.

"There was a lot of animosity toward the team being selected (as the Army's only official team) because you had two or three aviation demo teams who wanted something more comparable to the Blue Angels and Thunderbirds," he explained. "The thing that I think sold the team—and this

is just my opinion—is that you had individual personalities exposed to the public, as opposed to a select group of people in airplanes where they didn't get in contact with the public."

That close contact with the public was of great concern to the Golden Knights when considering new team members, Duffy said. Jumping ability was secondary to military bearing.

"We were looking for a good soldier who could represent the Army," he said. "It was easier to make a jumper than a soldier. And we got some who could outperform some of us in the air, but their attitudes were bad. They didn't fit."

When Duffy came to the team, it was divided into three five-man demo/comp teams, the Red, White and Blue Teams. He went to the White Team. They performed and competed as called upon. According to Duffy, each man had to be able to do everything in those days. When the team

was allowed to increase in size in 1963, it was divided into the Black and Gold Demonstration Teams and a Competition team. Finally, there was one team devoted to training for and competing in parachute competitions. Duffy went to the Comp Team.

"On a given day in 1965, I'd have to rate myself fifth or sixth (in Style & Accuracy) behind Coy McDonald, Bobby Letbetter, Dick Harmon and those guys," he said, pointing to an old photograph and naming faces. "But during that week (of the 1965 U.S. National Skydiving Championships)...well, that was my week. If it had happened a week later, one of them might have won."

But Duffy won just the same, becoming the 1965 overall national champion. The year before he had led the team to a second place finish at the first parachute competitions included in the Counseil Internationale du Sport Militare (CISM). He left the team in 1965 and returned in 1970 with a tour in Vietnam in between. In 1976, Duffy retired while serving as a first sergeant in the 1st Battalion, 505th Infantry of the 82d Airborne Division. Since retiring, he now works in aircraft maintenance, which he admits is a long way from his infantry background, but a job he enjoys. Now that he no longer jumps out of airplanes, he's content to work on them and keep them in the air for those who do.

"It's a great sport," he said of parachuting. "You meet lots of great people. Make lots of great friends. I did."

Sergeant Bill Jackson, current Style & Accuracy Team member, 1989 U.S. Nationals style champion.

SERGEANT BILL JACKSON

Whenever Sergeant Bill Jackson sets his mind to do something, he ensures no intricate detail is left out, whether it's drawing a lithographic print or parachute competition. That's why he has his artwork hanging in various offices in the Pentagon and gold medals hanging in the Golden Knights' trophy room.

Jackson is a National Style champion and the artist behind two lithographic prints presented by the team to its special friends. His first print, called "Knights Across America," depicts several of the many historic sites where the team has jumped, including the Statue of Liberty, Mount Rushmore, the St. Louis Arch and the Golden Gate Bridge. His most recent—a limited edition print called "Thirty Years of Excellence," captures on canvas what it would take thousands of words to say about the spirit driving the Golden Knights to strive for excellence, the same spirit that drives Bill Jackson.

Jackson is best described by friends and family as a "Christian country boy" from Drew, Mississippi. Before joining the Army in 1984 as a parachute rigger, Jackson earned an associate's degree in Graphic Design & Illustration at Delta Junior College, and he graduated from Ringling School of Art & Design. He maintained a good living as assistant art director of the Delta Design Group and as a part-time art teacher at Delta Junior College. But his self-imposed obligation to serve his country and his new-found hobby of skydiving affected his decision to enlist.

"I've always wanted to compete in some sport on a national level," he said, explaining his decision to join the Army with his sights on the Army Parachute Team. "If you really want something, you have to go after it. Dreams are made; they don't just happen."

His dream to compete on a national level was first realized when he made the team following Tryouts in 1985. After a season on the Knights' Black Demonstration Team, he tried out for and made the Style & Accuracy Team. At the 1988 U.S. Nationals, he managed to take second place overall. Later that summer, he took fifth place overall at the World Cup in France. Despite his personal ambition to compete and win, however, Jackson says he's particularly proud just to be an American soldier representing his country in world class competitions.

"I joined the Army because I love my country," he said emphatically. "I compete in international competitions for my country. That's why it's most important that the team wins, not the individual."

When he's not actively competing in a parachute competition or training for one, Jackson lends his artistic talents to the team, not only by painting special lithographic prints, but in the layout and design of team posters, brochures and even special-effect photo missions.

"I love the illusion that's created on a white piece of paper when you put different colors next to or on top of each other to come up with a painting that depicts the beauty of this great earth God gave us to enjoy," he explained, his eyes seeming to etch out a picture in the air. "I like my paintings to grow on you. The more you look at it, the more you should see."

Just prior to leaving for a parachute competition in Australia in November 1989, Jackson completed another print, this one as a commercial venture. He calls it "The Blackhawks" as, on first glance, it depicts two Black Hawk helicopters landing near a bunker. Jackson believes any soldier or former soldier who's ever endured the sudden blast of wind-blown sand and that extreme chill factor just to catch a ride from a chopper and escape enemy fire, or simply the elements themselves will be able to identify with and appreciate the rugged beauty of the moment he's captured on canvas.

"Making the rotor blades look as if they were spinning and actually lifting up the aircraft was challenging," the young soldier/artist said. "I wanted to make you feel the dust blowing in your face and your insides thumping with the pup-pup-pup of the blades over your head. To paint the sandbags, I had to go back to my basic training days. With every stroke I made on the bags, I imagined I was back there filling them one at a time. That's the only way I could have gotten them to look so heavy."

In addition to being an accomplished artist and a national parachute champion, Jackson is a self-taught interpreter for the hearing impaired. He says he took an interest in the subject and, like everything else he takes an interest in, he studied and practiced sign language until he had mastered it.

"First, I taught myself the symbols for all the letters of the alphabet," he explained, spelling out words with his fingers. "After I learned the alphabet, I learned to say words and phrases."

During the 1988 U.S. Nationals, a deaf man interested in the sport came out to the competition at Davis Airfield near Muskogee, Oklahoma. He'd hoped to learn something about the competition simply by watching, but Jackson made it even easier for him by explaining each event in this native language— sign language.

"I first linked up with him and began explaining the accuracy competition," Jackson said. "He gained a whole new appreciation for skydiving, and I really appreciated being able to help him."

Jackson probably doesn't realize just how many people he's helped by lending his various talents and time so generously, probably because people like Jackson don't keep a record of the lives they've touched, just the memories of the friends they've made. Whether he's serving as an interpreter, parachute competitor or artist, Jackson's personal drive to be his absolute best and his willingness to give his best to his team and his country represents the epitome of the American soldier.

In the minds of the youngsters who marvel at his parachuting achievements, to the art enthusiasts who admire his prints and to those hearing impaired Americans who've conversed with him through sign language, Sergeant Bill Jackson isn't just a soldier in the U.S. Army. He *is* the U.S. Army. By serving as an inspiration for so many in such various positive ways, he has helped the Army by fostering, if not restoring a sense of confidence in the kind of people who form America's military.

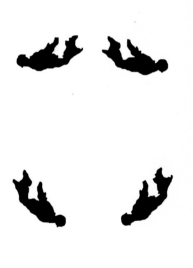

Staff Sergeant Jim Nipper, current Style & Accuracy Team member, 1986 U.S. Nationals accuracy champion.

STAFF SERGEANT JIM NIPPER

Most people couldn't imagine jumping into a hole 12,000 miles deep, but would concede that anyone who did would have lots of time to think about his decision to jump before reaching the bottom.

Staff Sergeant Jim Nipper began such a journey 15 years ago when he leaped from an aircraft two miles above the earth. Now, more than 6,000 jumps

later, he's traveled more than 12,000 miles through the air with only a small deceleration device to slow his rate of descent. And though he's had lots of time to think about his decision to make that first jump, he's never regretted his decision to become a freefall parachutist.

Nipper began skydiving in 1975. A short five years later, he had become so proficient in his craft, he was selected into the ranks of the world's most famous "skydivers," the Golden Knights. He began as a demonstration parachutist, then joined the Knights' Style & Accuracy Team, eventually becoming a national champion who's served on two U.S. Parachute Teams.

The Yorktown, Virginia native says he's very much at home in either event, style or accuracy. In 1986, he was the national accuracy champion with a total score of only one centimeter. In 1988, he took third place overall at the nationals. The following year, he became coach

for the team, leading them to a clean sweep of nearly every event, plus first, second and third place overall.

"I've made it my life ambition to win the world championships," Nipper said, admitting that goal has thus far evaded him.

Shortly after he was selected to his second U.S. Style & Accuracy Team in 1988, Nipper suffered a non-jump related injury. He broke his arm while climbing down an attic ladder back home at Fort Bragg. Regrettably, he did not go to Sweden that year.

But the win Nipper says he's looking for is not an individual or personal victory, but a team victory. Team victory at the 1986 world meet in Turkey simply wasn't there. Neither was it there for them in 1988.

"Overall country is what we're after," said Nipper, who decided to coach rather than compete, so his team would receive the full benefit of his experience rather than one individual's contribution as a competitor. ''The team winning the world championships is more important than individual gold medals.''

When he's not skydiving, Nipper enjoys shooting skeet or wind surfing, but he prefers a sport that offers competition.

That explains in part how he has done so well in the many national and international competitions in which he's been involved. ''Determination plays as big a part in a competition as talent,'' he says.

With 10 years as a Golden Knight, Nipper has a lot of seniority on the team. If he should ever be reassigned from the Army Parachute Team, he says he'll do everything he can to return. Regardless what the future holds, Nipper says he has no intention of ever giving up skydiving.

As an accelerated freefall instruction and tandem master, Nipper enjoys training other soldiers to become freefall parachutists, to help them experience

that feeling of flying miles above the earth with only a parachute to bring them safely back to earth.

RELATIVE WORKERS

Before a small crowd of dedicated parachutists who withstood a drizzling rain to witness an anti-climatic conclusion to a close competition, five Golden Knights (four competitors and an alternate) were awarded gold medals for the 4-way relative work event at the 1989 U.S. National Skydiving Championships. It was the sixth time the Knights had won the 4-way since 1981, the same year they won the world title in that event.

In the same ceremony, the Knights were honored as the overall winner of the Relative Work Championships—a repeat of the honor bestowed on them a few days earlier for the Style & Accuracy Championships. The previous day the team had won the 8-way event as expected, beating their

closest competitors by 46 points. It was the sixth time they won that event, too. In 1987 and later this same year, the Knights won the world title in the 8-way event. As such, several members of this team were already world champions when the national championships began.

Relative work competition is unlike Style & Accuracy competition in a very obvious way. The latter is basically an individual competition, even when scores are tallied for a team event. Relative work, however, requires teamwork on the ground and in the air. On the ground, each man practices his particular positions within the formations handed the team by the judges just before a round begins. He must memorize his precise body position in freefall relative to that of his teammates. As soon as the last hand grip is made, that formation is complete and they must move on to complete yet another formation. He must therefore know what position he must be in this time and the next time and the next time.

It takes practice, lots of practice. Most American civilian teams simply can't afford the time or the costs involved. The biggest competition comes from government-sponsored teams, such as the Soviets. The Golden Knights, being a U.S. Army team, can also be called a government-sponsored team. But the Soviets are more able to devote infinite funds and energies toward the development of their relative work team, which explains their tremendous improvements in the time it takes them to ''turn points.'' In 1987, they took third place behind the French. In 1989, they took second place only five points behind the U.S. The Knights averaged 13.8 points per round after 10 rounds. The Soviets averaged 13.3 points per round.

Despite the close competition given them by the Soviets, however, it should be noted the Knights turned more than 20 points in a single practice round before the competition began. The competition may be getting better, but so are the Golden Knights.

''We'd been together as a team for two years,'' explained **Staff Sergeant Jim Coffman**. ''Although we didn't concentrate on the 4-way event for the nationals, we had the advantage of experience going for us.''

The close bonds developed between men who work together for a common goal can be found in any size military unit, and the Golden Knights, afterall, are a military unit—one with a mission to defeat their challengers on the field of competition. The grounds gained in such victories cannot be measured simply by medals and trophies brought home. The confidence each man or woman develops in themselves and their teammates is the real reward. For such people return to regular Army units to inspire others to achieve the same high standards. They may prove to be invaluable in times of crisis, or in delicate situations where leadership is needed. The Knights are those kind of men and women. At the conclusion of the '89 world championships, the Knights lost nearly half of their relative work team to reassignments Army-wide. ''The team's loss,'' explained one member, ''is the Army's gain.''

The closeness between members of the Knights' Relative Work Team is evidenced not only by their national and world titles, but the nicknames given to each other signifying a special friendship, names like: Bonefish, J.C., Scooter, Raff and Goob. ''One member's personal problems and triumphs is every member's personal problems and triumphs,'' explained **Sergeant First Class Andy Gerber**, former team leader of the Knights' Relative Work Team.

Gerber noted that at

the conclusion of the '89 Nationals, **Sergeant Todd Lorenzo** was recognized by the U.S. Parachute Association for his outstanding support throughout the competition as a freefall photographer providing air-to-air video coverage to the judges. The USPA's recognition was amplified by his teammates—particularly **Sergeant Kevin Peyton**, the team's other freefall photographer, who also supported the competition as a freefall photographer. Peyton and the others congratulated their teammate/friend with both a handshake and a hug.

According to the team's operations sergeant, **Sergeant First Class Bill Brown**, members of the Relative Work Team are the most physically fit on the entire team. All Golden Knights exceed Army standards on the Army Physical Fitness Readiness Test, with an overall team average of 288.8 on a test where 300 is the maximum possible score—a test requiring a 30-year-old

man (the average age of relative workers) to do 82 pushups in two minutes, 79 situps in two minutes and complete a two mile run in 13 minutes, 18 seconds. The 10-man Relative Work Team averages a near-perfect 299 points.

Relative workers also tend to be the most athletic. **Sergeant Willie Lee** enjoys hang gliding whenever their schedule allows it. **Staff Sergeant Paul Rafferty** appreciates the challenge of a triathlon competition consisting of a marathon run, swim and cycle race. Rafferty's participation in parachute competitions and triathlons led to his being selected as Fort Bragg's Athlete of the Year for 1989. Other members, like Staff **Sergeants Scott Rhodes** and Coffman and **Sergeant Craig Girard**, appreciate things like music or woodcraft. **Sergeant First Class Chris Wagner**, the team leader, devotes the majority of his spare time toward bettering his military career. A recent graduate of Special

Forces' Operations & Intelligence (O&I) course, he also earned a reserve commission as a first lieutenant during his off duty time. Their interests outside the workplace may vary, but the intensity with which they thrust themselves into life is the same for all. They're competitors to the core. That's why they're world champions.

Sergeant First Class Andy Gerber, former Relative Work Team Leader, three-time world champion and 1988 Golden Knight of the Year.

SERGEANT FIRST CLASS ANDY GERBER

When he was selected to be a Golden Knight following Tryouts in 1978, Sergeant First Class Andy Gerber compared his being a member of the Army Parachute Team to being a full-time Olympian. Ten years later, he became a part of the Olympic games as he and five other Golden Knight teammates joined another 24 relative work world champions in freefall to form the five Olympic rings (three rings over two) above the Olympic stadium in Seoul, South Korea.

By that time, 1988, Gerber was a two-time world champion. The following year, he'd win his third world title in relative work, for a total of one in 4-way and two in 8-way. He's the only parachutist in history to win world titles in two separate relative work events, much less heap a third world title to his credit. But competition, he says, is a way of life. Most of all, Gerber firmly believes any competition worth entering is worth winning.

"I don't think much of second place," he said, grinning, but he meant it. "Seriously, you're not competing if you're not trying to win."

From his arrival at team tryouts in October 1978, to his departure in January 1990 for an overseas assignment that would send him back to Korea for a slightly longer stay, Gerber amassed nearly 8,500 freefall parachute jumps, or roughly 116 hours spent in freefall. Freefall hours are measured from the time the jumper leaves the aircraft to the time he opens his parachute, which is usually about 60 seconds from 12,000 feet. In this country, Gerber is in third place as far as the amount of time he holds in freefall, but don't ask him how he feels about being third in the nation. (Remember, he doesn't care much about second place.) He has no comment about third, or at least not one he'll express to "strangers, journalists, non-jumpers and other strange people."

Gerber attended high school at the New Mexico Military Institute in Anthony, New Mexico. Upon his graduation in 1968, he attended college for two years at New Mexico State University. But in 1973 he was introduced to the love of his life—skydiving—and school "took a back burner." Three years later, he enlisted in the Army as an electronic security specialist, but continued to hone his jumping skills by joining a civilian sport parachute club.

"I knew about the Golden Knights before I came in," he admitted. "I mean, everybody had heard of their reputation in competitions. I thought I'd try out for the team two years after I joined the Army."

At one point during tryouts, he thought he might be cut from the team. Every tryout, he believes, has this feeling at some point during the program, although few have come to the team with his qualifications. When he was certain he was about to be "axed" from tryouts, Gerber wrote a note to the tryout cadre asking them not to release him before they had the opportunity to jump a C-141 scheduled for the following Monday. A chance to "tailgate" a C-141 was something no self-respecting parachutist would want to miss. So as not to miss his chance, he wrote:

"Roses are red and grow in the sun, Please don't axe me before we jump the '141."

Gerber made the team (despite having his poetic license revoked!) and went straight to the Knights' fledgling Relative Work Team. Little more than two years later, his contribution to the team added to the Golden Knights' sterling reputation, as he was part of the Knights' 4-way team which won the world championships held that year at Zephyrhills, Florida. Between the world championship in 4-way and his first 8-way championship in 1987, Gerber helped the Knights earn "piles" of national and various other world titles in relative work at such competitions as the World Cup and Pan American Cup. In fact, he speculates that if he was required to wear all the medals he's won around his neck at one time, he wouldn't be able to stand up.

"You don't think about the medals," he explained. "You just think about winning."

Winning was something his teammates and chain of command could count on as long as he was team leader of the Knights' Relative Work Team. In fact, his reputation as a tough competitor and unquestionable expertise in relative work enabled him to be team leader even though he was not the senior ranking NCO on the RW team. In competition, even in the military, rank has far less to do with the success or failure of their mission than ability. And Gerber was a man who's proven ability was so evident, his selection as team leader was simply the most logical choice.

Looking back on his long, competitive career with the Golden Knights, Gerber admits to having one regret. For as long as there has been an Army Parachute Team, there has been talk that parachuting might some day be included as an exhibition sport in the Olympics and not simply as an exhibition to entertain the spectators.

The country hosting the Olympics has the right to select a certain number of exhibition sports, and the Spanish Olympic Committee was in Seoul in 1988 to watch the parachute exhibition. The 1989 World Championships were even held in Spain. And yet, the committee once again decided against including parachuting as an Olympic exhibition sport.

"Money talks," Gerber said tersely. "And we just don't have the financial backing to get skydiving entered into the Olympics."

According to Gerber, the sports to be included as exhibition sports in the Olympics are actually dictated to the host country by the Olympic sponsors. The television rights to the 1992 Olympics were bought at a phenomenal cost by an American television network, one very much concerned that the exhibition sports at "their" Olympics would be a commercial success back home. For this reason, "softball" will be an exhibition sport in 1992. Parachuting will have to wait.

If parachuting is part of the 1996 Olympics, Gerber plans to be a part of it, even though he'll be in his 40's by then. He explains that if he's not a competitor, he'll coach. Competitor or coach, one thing is certain, if he's part of the Olympics, this Olympian Knight will ensure his team is victorious.

Staff Sergeant Scott Rhodes, current Relative Work Team assistant team captain and two-time world champion.

STAFF SERGEANT SCOTT RHODES

"I was one of those kids who didn't play any sports because I was just too skinny," retorted one of parachuting's heavyweights, Staff Sergeant Scott Rhodes.

When he graduated from Pittsburg's Allderdice High School in 1977, Rhodes had never experienced the thrill of competition. Today, he's a two-time world champion, not to mention having earned eight national and four world cup gold medals. Shrugging his shoulders, he says he has no idea how many second and third place honors he's won. No one, including the athlete, remembers who came in second second, Rhodes said.

Rhodes is an indirect fire infantryman. That is, he trains and supervises the operation of 60mm, 81mm and 4.2-inch mortars. He joined the Army for no other reason than to better himself—better, in that he was working as a landscaping laborer after high school—a job offering him little chance for advancement and absolutely no chance to see the world. Rhodes enlisted in 1978 and was assigned to the 82d Airborne Division at Fort Bragg. Two years later, he began skydiving.

"I saw the Golden Knights jump at the 82d (Airborne Division) Museum," he explained. "'Hmmmm,' I told myself, 'that's something I ought to give a try.' So, I joined the 82d (Sport Parachute) Club that weekend."

His training included five static line jumps, with which he was now thoroughly familiar. It also required him to make one 'hop and pop' jump and three each 5-second, 10-second, 15-second and 20-second delay jumps. During each of these jumps, Rhodes had to perform various turns and maneuvers to ultimately become freefall qualified.

In little more than a year, he made 450 freefall jumps. With these jumps and three years experience as a paratrooper, he felt confident to try out for the Army Parachute Team. Rhodes' confidence in his abilities as a parachutist and as a soldier were well-founded. He was selected and assigned to the Black Demonstration Team. His most memorable demonstration jumps include the opening ceremonies at the Indianapolis 500 in 1982 and jumping the American flag into a USFL football game in 1983. By then, however, Rhodes was no longer a demonstrator, but a member of the Knights' Relative Work Team.

"Both world championships (1987 and 1989) were tough," he said. "But I'd have to say 1989 was the toughest. It's easy to become Number One; it's hard to stay Number One."

Rhodes currently serves as the assistant team captain, now having more than 6,200 jumps, or about 96 hours in freefall to his credit. He's also a nationally rated judge, an AFF (accelerated freefall) Instructor and a parachute rigger.

And no longer does he allow his weight and body dimensions to keep him from entering other sports competitions. In 1988 he entered the Marine Corps Marathon, a 26-mile ordeal that he completed in three hours, 18 minutes. He ran the marathon on Saturday at Camp Lejeune, which is about 120 miles from

Fort Bragg, then had to train Monday morning for an upcoming parachute competition.

"I was sore, you can believe that," he said, grinning. "But I trained just the same."

When he isn't jumping or running, Rhodes enjoys playing the drums—a hobby his wife, Trisha, has put on hold for a while, thanks to the recent arrival of their newborn daughter.

As a paratrooper in the 82d Airborne Division, Rhodes had an opportunity to see parts of the world few people have ever seen (parts of the world few people would want to see for that matter—deserts, jungles and even glaciers). But as a Golden Knight, he has toured the United States as a parachute demonstrator and competitor and competed in six foreign nations, including France, England, Spain, Saudi Arabia, Brazil and Australia. He's had an opportunity to see the world and prove to himself, if no one else, that being "skinny"

didn't exclude him from participating in sports.

Captain Glenn Bangs, former Relative Work Team leader, 1981 world champion and Golden Knight of the Year.

CAPTAIN GLENN BANGS

From the days of the early STRAC Team, to the present Golden Knights, dozens of soldiers have left the Army Parachute Team as enlisted soldiers and become commissioned officers, but only four of

them ever returned to the team afterwards. Captain Glenn Bangs is one of them.

Bangs, a man with two hometowns—Reading, Pennsylvania and Richmond, Virginia, began his military career as a draftee. He was a sophomore at Stroudsburg College when he received his "invitation" from the Army in October 1972.

"That was nearly 18 years ago," Bangs said as he adjusted a bronze Golden Knight statuette on the front of his desk. An inscription at the base of it read: SFC GLENN G. BANGS, WORLD CHAMPION GOLDEN KNIGHT, JAN 77-APR 82. "Looking back on it, I've thoroughly enjoyed it all."

Bangs said he chose a 3-year Airborne/Ranger option over the 2-year, go-anywhere without an option draft. Following Ranger School, he was assigned to the 2nd Ranger Battalion at Fort Lewis, Washington, then the 1st Ranger Battalion at Fort Stewart, Georgia. It was at Fort

Stewart that Bangs was introduced to his two favorite hobbies—scuba diving and skydiving.

In 1976, Bangs tried out for and was selected to become a Golden Knight. At the time, he had less than 500 jumps. Today he has over 5,000.

"I was interested in sequential relative work competition," he said. "But that competition was just getting started back then and the senior guy on the team got all the slots on the RW Team."

In 1979 he got his chance to become a relative worker. Two years later, he and teammates **Andy Gerber, Bob Finn, Mark Gabriel** and **Mike Devault**, won both the national and world title in the 4-way relative work event. That same year his teammates voted him as the Golden Knight of the Year. The following year, he left the team to attend Officer Candidate School at Fort Benning, Georgia. At the time, he felt his years with the Golden Knights were ended forever due to the limited number of officer positions on the team.

He remained at Fort Benning after OCS and the Officer Infantry Basic Course, serving with the Airborne School, Infantry School and the 3rd Ranger Battalion. In the latter assignment, he served as a Special Operations Officer responsible for the training, deployment and utilization of HALO personnel, including HALO jumpmaster, snipers, assault climber, combat divers and scout swimmers. During this time, he also served as trainer and coach of the Silver Wings, Fort Benning's parachute demonstration team.

Bangs was completing his bachelor's at Columbus College when he learned about a possible opening for an operations officer back at his old alma mater, the Golden Knights. On June 9, 1988, the day after graduating, he returned home by signing in at team headquarters at Fort Bragg.

"This assignment is considered a 'pearl' by officers and enlisted alike," he explained. "I feel it's a privilege to be back with the most professional soldiers in the Army."

Shortly after returning to the team, Bangs left for Korea with several members of the current RW Team. To add to the colorful opening ceremonies of the 1988 Summer Olympics in Seoul, Bangs and five of his teammates joined 24 other world champions in freefall to form the five Olympic rings over the stadium. The Knights, appropriately enough, made up the gold ring.

The following summer, Bangs and former 4-way world champion **Bob Finn** teamed up again with **Sergeants Jeff** and **John Steele** (not related) and **Jake Brown** of the Gold Demonstration Team to form a 4-way team to compete in the Bali Indonesian International Skydiving Championships.

"We only had...at max, 120 training jumps," he said, eyes squinting. "But it was like I'd gone away for a long time and come back home. And it was as if Sergeant Finn and I had never stopped working together. We were still on the same wavelength.''

Bangs said he and Finn gave the newly formed team their experience, whereas the three demonstrators (two were competitors, one was an alternate/freefall photographer) cooperated with their enthusiasm and willingness to learn. Their team not only took first place in relative work, but third place overall.

In two years, Bangs will be eligible for retirement, but he's not making any plans. As far as his being one of only four Golden Knights to leave the team as an enlisted soldier and return as an officer, he points out that a famous ancestor, Confederate Colonel John S. Mosby was an enlisted man before General J.E.B. Stewart made him an officer in his calvary. Mosby's Raiders, he points out, were forerunners to today's Ranger

units. Mosby himself would have probably made a fine Golden Knight!

At least his great-great grandson has proven to be a fine Golden Knight—twice over!

Sergeant Willie Lee, current Relative Work Team member, two-time world champion.

SERGEANT WILLIE LEE

Omro, Wisconsin native William ''Willie'' Lee, has always enjoyed the great outdoors, high adventure and the thrill of competi-

tion. As a boy, he enjoyed snow skiing in the winter and water skiing in the summer. Such action sports presented a challenge that aroused something in him which refused to go away. He still enjoys skiing, but nowadays he finds his adventures, his challenges, at a slightly higher altitude—at about 13,000 feet where the only thing snowy is a few puffs of soft white clouds.

Lee is a world champion—a two-time world champion at that. On September 17, 1988, Lee helped set the stage for the world's greatest athletes as part of the opening ceremonies of the 1988 Summer Olympics. He earned the right to be a part of that parachute exhibition for his part in the Golden Knights' 1986 and 1988 World Cup title in 8-way Relative Work and its 1987 World Championship title in that event. A year after the Olympics, Lee confirmed his right to be included among the world's finest athletes by again winning the world title in the 8-way event.

Lee started skydiving shortly after graduating from Omro High School in 1979. He attended the University of Wisconsin at Oshkosh for three semesters, but skydiving began to be such an important part of his life, he lost interest in academics.

"My whole life began to evolve around skydiving," Lee explained. "By the time I joined the Army in '82, I already had 600 jumps."

He now has nearly 6,000 jumps and a significant stockpile of medals from national and international parachute competitions. Although the standard tour with the Army Parachute Team is three years, Lee has been helping the team to win U.S. and world titles since 1984. And, he says emphatically, if possible, he intends to stay with the Golden Knights at least until the 1992 Summer Olympics, where the Knights will once again be involved in a parachute exhibition.

"Competition gets to be an addiction after a while," he said. "You get a certain kind of adrenalin rush, that... well, if you can control it the way we (the Golden Knights) have, you can use that adrenal energy to your advantage."

Lee harnesses his own adrenal energy for the Army's advantage, not only to win medals in parachute competitions, but as a well-disciplined, highly trained soldier. Lee, a parachute rigger, emphasizes that his selection to and retention on the Army Parachute Team was and is contingent on his performance as a soldier, as well as his performance in competition. And because he's basically working in his job specialty every day— packing and maintaining parachuting equipment—the Army is in no hurry to reassign him.

Only a few months prior to his participation in the 1988 Olympics ceremonies, Lee added hang gliding to his high adventure hobbies. The initial investment in the sport, the hang glider itself, was about the same as his initial investment in skydiving, Lee explained. However, after buying his equipment, he now needs only a high enough place to launch his glider and a safe place to land. There's no need for (or expense of) an aircraft. He "plays" tirelessly with his hang glider in his off hours, working toward the day when he will be good enough to participate in hang gliding competitions.

When asked if hang gliding will ever replace skydiving, Lee gives an emphatic "no." His life still evolves around that sport, even though he's conquered about all there is to conquer in the sport, with two world championship titles and being part of a military world record. In February 1989, Lee and 44 Golden Knight teammates set a military record for the number of jumpers linking together in freefall to form a giant star.

"The only thing harder than winning, is

remaining the winner," Lee said, almost with remorse. "If that's the only challenge left for me, I'll take it. I need a challenge to survive."

With a large changeover of personnel on the Knights' Relative Work Team after the 1989 World Championships, Lee found himself challenged as a leader. His experience as a world champion will be called upon again and again to help train new members of the team so the Knights will be able to remain winners.

THE AVIATORS

They called themselves "Team 6" because the aviation section of the Army Parachute Team was the sixth section, or team within the Knights. Six warrant and one commissioned officer pilots are responsible for getting the parachute demonstrators to and from show sites and for supporting both comp and demo teams during training. These pilots, however, would never be able to get off the ground if not for the support of their crew chiefs and maintenance teams.

"They're the first ones (to arrive) in the morning and the last ones to leave at night," said **Captain James Daley**, former OIC of the aviation section. "They keep us flying."

Golden Knight crew chiefs, says Daley, average about eight years military experience, and the pilots themselves are some of the most experienced pilots in the Army. Nearly all are qualified to fly both fixed wing and rotary wing aircraft. Each pilot has at least 5,000 flying hours, many of them with combat flying experience. One former Golden Knight pilot, **Chief Warrant Officer Michael Novosel**, was awarded the Medal of Honor for his valor and gallantry as a "dust-off" pilot in Vietnam. In fact, some of the most highly decorated soldiers on the Army Parachute Team are aviators, including the current commander, **Lieutenant Colonel Kirk Knight**, who spent two tours in Vietnam as an infantryman, went to Officer Candidate School and flight school, then returned to Vietnam as a "spotter" pilot.

According to John Hollis, the first aircraft organic to the team was a Twin Otter and a DC-3 (later redesignated C-47). By 1975, only the C-47 was still being used, and it was replaced that year by the YC-7A Caribou, which became the principle aircraft supporting the two demo teams. Between 1975 and 1985 when the Knights replaced the Caribou with the Fokker, they added two U21's to their fleet to support the comp teams. The F27 Fokker (now redesignated C-31) is a Dutch-made, twin engine turbo-prop aircraft used extensively in this country and Europe as a commuter plane. The Knights use it to commute to air shows around the country, but they favor it most for being what it truly is—a fine jump platform.

The aviation section is the only section not located with the rest of the team, but for obvious reasons. Team 6 shares a hanger at Simmons Army Airfield, which is about five miles from the team area. According to the section's NCOIC, **Staff Sergeant Jeff Geyer**, plans are in the making to move the aviation section to Pope Air Force Base, which is barely a mile from the team area. Other plans in the offing include the search for a replacement to the U21's which could feasibly be used both in training and taking the comp teams on the road. That search, says Daley, will be long and thorough. More than half of the Golden Knights' annual budget goes in support of the aviation section. And although the purchase of a new airplane is a one-time sunken cost, not really effecting the annual budget, the maintenance and fuel cost of any plane selected will greatly influence that selection.

The importance of the aircraft and their teammates in the aviation section is never forgotten by the demonstrators and competitors, explained **Sergeant First Class Bill Brown**, NCOIC of the team's operations section.

"Team members sometimes joke with the pilots about landings so bumpy they can be logged twice in their flight logs, and with the crew chiefs about washing the wings," said Brown. "But every man on this team knows that every time he gets in one of our planes, his pilots and crew chief are among the best in the Army. I think the aviation guys know they're appreciated. If they don't, I'll call 'em up and tell 'em so right now!"

He did. Brown called Geyer to tell him how much he appreciated their support, then informed him that two of his soldiers were scheduled for a physical training test the following morning and that one of the U21's would be needed to support

weekend training by the Style & Accuracy Team in Raeford, North Carolina. Brown says the aviation and headquarters section identify well with the job each does—a job very similar in that both "exist to support the demonstration and competition teams." Geyer, who used to work in operations and is himself a former demonstrator and a former helicopter pilot, serves as a welding link between the aviation section and the rest of the team. He, his crew chiefs and the team's pilots know that without them, the Golden Knights wouldn't be able to show off before the crowds. And with the utmost humility, they ensure the team accomplishes its mission by keeping their teammates airborne.

Captain James Daley, former aviation section leader and pilot.

CAPTAIN JAMES DALEY

He lay face down on the wet ground near an isolated airstrip in a pouring, icy rain. A 70-pound rucksack dug into the back of his neck as the young sergeant tried to determine what part of his weary body hurt most, his sick-of-C-rations stomach, or his aching infantry feet.

The unmistakable pup-pup-pup of a helicopter squadron could be heard above the rumble of distant thunder. As quickly as the choppers landed, a crew chief inside of each slid back the doors, inviting a platoon of shivering paratroopers to come in out of the rain.

The young sergeant, James Daley, quickly gave his men the signal to load. As they ran at a double-time to their assigned "bird," Daley couldn't help noticing the pilots in the cockpit. They were dry and most probably, quite warm too.

"That's for me," he told himself.

The Warren, Ohio native made a decision right then to change the course of his military career from enlisted infantry paratrooper to aviation officer. Of course, he'd have to get accepted to and graduate from Officer Candidate School (OCS) and flight school, but those details would be worked out later. The decision to "get out of the rain" was momentous enough for the moment.

Daley is a captain, formerly the senior pilot and OIC of the Golden Knights' aviation section. In addition to supervising Team 6 with its six warrant officer pilots and supporting crews with a fleet of four aircraft, Daley augmented the team as a pilot for both air shows and training.

"Most Army aviators average about 200 flying hours a year," Daley explained. "Golden Knight pilots average about 500 flying hours a year."

On September 25, 1989, Daley returned home, or at least, close to his home—Greenville, Pennsylvania—for the 75th anniversary of the Army's adoption of the parachute. He was the pilot for the Knights' Gold Demonstration Team, who demonstrated what the Army had done with the parachute in 75 years of researching uses for it and ways of improving on it.

Daley says he elected to fly that particular show himself rather than send one of his other pilots because Greenville is so close to Warren (right across the border) and because he attended Thiel College there, graduating with honors in 1986 through a degree completion program.

"Greenville is just as much my hometown as Warren," he said. "It was a little like waving to the hometown folks when we did the fly-by."

When he left the 82d Airborne Division to attend OCS and Fixed Wing Flight School, Daley knew his future would be more technically demanding with even greater responsibilities. As an infantry squad leader, he was responsible for the lives of his men in combat. He had to train them thoroughly and always make clear, tactically sound decisions. But as a pilot, he's knows he's solely responsible for the lives of his passengers.

"Pilots are more than just glorified taxi drivers," Daley said. "I know that every time I climb in that cockpit, there's a group of soldiers aboard that plane depending on me

to get them to their destination safely and bring them home the same way."

Daley explained that when the headaches and pressures of flying start to get to him, he just thinks back to that cold, rainy day when he decided to become a pilot.

"Hey, it beats walking," he laughed. "Seriously though, I really love to fly, and, well, it may sound corny, but I'm proud to say I flew for the Golden Knights. I think they're the best bunch of soldiers in the Army."

When he retires from the Army in just a few more years, Daley plans to pursue a second career as a civilian pilot. And though he says he will never regret his decision to fly, he'll always treasure his "good 'ol days" in the airborne infantry.

Chief Warrant Officer (retired) Butch Richister, pilot.

CHIEF WARRANT OFFICER FOUR BUTCH RICHISTER

The Air Medal is awarded for meritorious achievement, service or heroism while participating in flight against an armed enemy. Chief Warrant Officer Four Woodrow "Butch" Richister knows the criteria for this award by heart. With 1,039 combat hours flying in 425 combat missions in Vietnam, Richister has been awarded not one, but 18 Air Medals.

Richister enlisted in the Army in 1968 under a special option to attend the Fixed Wing Flight School. The "option," he says, was simple. He could successfully complete the course and become a warrant officer-pilot, or he could fail the course and become an 11B-infantryman.

"The alternative of being a 'grunt' wasn't used against us as a threat," said Richister who retired December 1988. "But it was a definite motivating factor."

Richister was born in Hattisburg, Mississippi, but says he grew up as an Army "brat" in Columbus, South Carolina. His father, Woodrow L. Richister, retired at Fort Jackson as an ordnance supply warrant officer. However, he says his father hardly influenced his decision to enter the Army.

"I started flying when I was still in high school," Richister said. "I attended a business school for a couple of years, but I wasn't satisfied. I wanted to fly for a living, and the Army offered me the quickest way to get started."

At age 22, Richister accepted the Army's offer and, at the same time, the responsibility of a family. He and his wife, Bettie Anne, now have two boys, Stan and Chris. Their oldest son, Stan, is enrolled in Air Force ROTC, and, following in his father's footsteps, has recently obtained his private pilot's license.

Richister doesn't deny influencing his son's affinity for flying (although he might voice some displeasure about his choice of service!).

The Air Medals only partially testify to Richister's devotion to duty and service to the Army. Upon his retirement, he had completed two tours with the Golden Knights. He'd flown approximately 8,000 hours without an accident, with half those hours in service to the Army Parachute Team. In 10 demonstration seasons, he'd flown for over 1,500 air shows, releasing over 65,000 jumpers before millions of spectators.

"The Knights' aviation section probably flies more than any other section on (Fort) Bragg or Pope (Air Force Base)," he said. "During my last year, we flew over 600 hours."

Aside from his tenure in Vietnam and two tours with the Golden Knights, Richister served two tours in Korea, and he attended a number of other flight schools, including the Rotary Wing Qualification Course. He also completed both an associate's and bachelor's degree in liberal studies through the University of the State of New York while he was on active duty.

Richister was noted by former Golden Knights commander, **Colonel Bruce Wicks**, as the driving force behind the decision to replace the Knights' old YC-7A caribou with the F27 Fokker in December 1985. He personally designed the paint job for the Fokker with its prominent black and gold finish.

"It was both reward-ing and frustrating," he said, summing up his long military career. "In all walks of life, you have to take the good with the bad. I take a lot of personal pride in hav-ing served my country in Vietnam, as my father did in World War II. I'm also proud to have been able to help the para-chute team in the ac-quisition of its new air-craft."

Upon his retirement, Richister may have stopped flying for the Army, but he didn't stop flying. He says he doesn't look forward to "that" type of retire-ment. Richister now flies for a civilian commuter airline.

Chief Warrant Officer Four Luis Jimenez, pilot and 1988 Aviator of the Year.

CHIEF WARRANT OFFICER FOUR LUIS R. JIMENEZ

Calling himself a "cranky old W4," Chief Warrant Officer Four Luis R. Jimenez says he was more surprised than anyone when his Golden Knight team-mates elected him as the 1988 Aviator of the Year.

"I like things to run efficiently, and I like the Army," Jimenez ex-plained matter-of-factly.

"I tend to be particular about details, which sometimes rubs people the wrong way."

But any friction he may have caused by demanding the best from his subordinates and peers only resulted in genuine respect and admiration. At the presentation of the Aviator of the Year award during the Knights' annual reunion dinner, December 10, 1988, Jimenez received a standing ovation from current, former and honorary teammates.

That respect, said his former supervisor, **Cap-tain James Daley**, was well-earned over an il-lustrious 20 year career in Army aviation. Jimenez enlisted June 1970, just in time to make the last class for the Initial Entry Fixed Wing Flight Course. Later, he also attended the Rotary Wing Qualification Course.

Jimenez has since served two tours in Korea, as well as an 18 month stint in El Salva-dor, where he was responsible for training Salvadorian helicopter pilots and developing helicopter squadrons for the Salvadorian Army. He not only trained their pilots, he trained their pilots to be instructors so they could train other Salvadorians.

Being a native of San Juan, Puerto Rico, Jimenez speaks fluent Spanish, which made him a tremendous asset to the Salvadorian Army as an advisor during their on-going civil war. Like many other Americans who have served in advisory roles for our allies, he sometimes found himself caught up in their conflict.

"I don't think the Army called it a combat tour," he said, grinning. "But I got shot at quite a bit."

Jimenez also served as an instructor at Fort Rucker, Alabama, where he taught the Instructor Qualification Course for UH-1H and OH-58 helicopters, the Rotary Wing Qualification Course, the Tactics/Nap of the Earth and Night Vision Goggle Instructor Courses and, finally, the Fixed Wing Qualification Course.

On a later tour at Fort Rucker, he was selected to serve as a Worldwide Aviation Standards Pilot, responsible for evaluating Army aviators around the world. In 1986 he left an assignment with 7th Special Forces Group to fly for the Army Parachute Team. Three show seasons and 1,500 flying hours later, his teammates concluded he had done more than anyone else to enhance the team's image and promote the Army to the American people.

Describing himself as an athletic type with a love for outdoor adventure, Jimenez fit right in with the Golden Knights from the start. His work, flying, is also one of his hobbies. Other hobbies include scuba diving, cycling and, appropriately enough, skydiving. In 1982 he won first place in the accuracy competition at the Military Nationals held at Fort Bragg.

Jimenez attributes his career success to the support he receives at home from his wife, Helen, and their four

children, Nanette, Marette, Clay and Candice.

"Helen has the hardest job," he said. "She works full-time, keeps house and puts four kids off to school every day. And does a great job of it! It doesn't help that I'm gone most of the time with the team."

He emphasized his praise of his wife with some emotion, noting the stress and other untold demands on Army wives. With his family in mind, Jimenez says he's already considering retirement so he can spend more time with them. Even when he retires from Army aviation, however, he intends to continue flying as a civilian pilot.

Staff Sergeant Jeff Geyer, aviation section NCOIC and 1989 Aviator of the Year.

STAFF SERGEANT JEFF GEYER

Staff Sergeant Jeff Geyer is an outdoorsman extraordinare. That is, he's not only a hunter and fisherman, he has a sense of humor and a keen ability to express it through his hunting and fishing tales. After all, no outdoorsman is sufficiently skilled in his craft until he can make a boring, unsuccessful adventure sound exciting—even to other outdoorsmen who know better!

During some downtime, following an airshow in Montana in 1989, Geyer and Golden Knight teammate **Sergeant Eric Folkstadt** decided to try their luck at trout fishing. When his line became entangled on the tip of an overhanging tree limb, Geyer reached out to free it, only to fall headlong into the rushing stream. His hip waders filled with water, pulling him under and along with the current to where he was passing by Folkstadt.

''Jeff!'' His teammate approached Geyer, his voice relaying his apparent annoyance with someone so rude as to swim through his fishing hole. Because Jeff was laughing as he thrashed about to get back to shore, Folkstadt didn't think Geyer was in any danger, or at least, not too much danger. ''What are you doing?!''

''Drowning?'' Geyer answered, matter-of-factly. ''Do ya mind?''

As soon as he reached the shallows of a bend, Geyer dragged himself to shore, emptied several gallons of icy stream water from his waders, then returned fishing. Folkstadt managed to catch a few keeper-sized trout, but Geyer wasn't even lucky enough to catch a cold!

He does have a few trophies to his credit, however, including a 300-pound, 9-point white tail taken in Montana in 1988. A full month before the close of North Carolina's 1989 deer season, Geyer had already reached his limit of five deer. But hunting is not the only outdoor sport in which he's made marked achievements.

Geyer is a helicopter pilot with over 1,100 flying hours, 700 of which as pilot in command. He's also a skydiver with nearly 800 freefall parachute jumps. Unlike hunting and fishing (which he's enjoyed from the cradle) Geyer began flying and skydiving after joining the Army.

In 1975, after graduating from Southside Christian High School in

Greenville, South Carolina, the man who was to become the Golden Knights' resident trophy hunter was hunting for a job. He found one as an indirect fire infantryman (mortars) assigned with the 24th Infantry Division at Fort Stewart, Georgia. After two years as "a leg," Geyer decided to "go airborne," so he volunteered to go next door to the 1st Ranger Battalion. There he was able to not only go to Airborne School, but also Ranger School, earning both jump wings and a Ranger tab.

By 1979 Geyer felt he was spending entirely too much time on the ground, so he went to Warrant Officer Flight School. Two years later while flying a UH-1 helicopter during a training exercise in Germany, he hit some high tension wires that couldn't be seen because they blended in with the treeline. Geyer broke his back during the resulting crash. While he was recovering from his injuries, he took up skydiving.

"I wasn't able to fly at the time, and I hadn't made a jump since I left the Ranger Battalion," he explained. "I love jumping as much as I love flying."

That combination—jumping and flying—would ultimately lead to his being selected by his teammates as the 1989 Golden Knight Aviator of the Year. But first he had to get on the team, which wasn't going to be easy since he wasn't an enlisted soldier (a prerequisite to coming to tryouts).

When his warrant commitment ended September 1984, Geyer enlisted and applied for tryouts. At the time, he admits, he thought tryouts were actually a "formality," and his coming to the Army Parachute Team was part of his enlistment agreement.

"I didn't know when I came to tryouts that most of the people got cut," he laughed. "But, looking back on it, I still think it was worth the gamble."

He was selected to the team, despite breaking his ankle during the last week of tryouts. At the end of his first show season, he severely injured his knee and reinjured his back. That injury resulted in his being medically grounded from flying and jumping. He could have left the Army with medical benefits, but chose to stay with the Golden Knights by working as the assistant operations NCOIC. Two years later, he took over the aviation section as the NCOIC, responsible for all the enlisted members of his section, their training and supervision. He's also the one who ensures the team's aircraft are always prepared to fly. According to his first sergeant, Jeff Moon, Geyer's experience as both a pilot and parachute demonstrator make him an invaluable asset to both his section and the entire team.

Geyer credits his parents, Reverend Jimmie Geyer and his wife, Jean, with his optimistic attitude, love of the outdoors and moral character. He may no longer be able to fly or jump, "at least" he now has more free time to hunt and fish. But even there, his ethical standards reflect his Christian rearing.

"If I don't eat it, or if there's no one I can donate the meat to, I won't hunt it," he explained.

On one occasion, however, Geyer was forced to shoot something out of defense rather than for food. While squirrel hunting on the northeast side of Fort Bragg in 1986, Geyer found he was the one being hunted. A pack of wild dogs had been following him for some time. He could hear them in the thicket but couldn't see them. They wouldn't dare attack a man, he told himself.

"I heard the shrubs erupt," he said excitedly, waving his hands in the air and standing as if there was a campfire between him and his listeners. "Out came this Doberman heading straight for me, growling...which told me he wasn't coming over to be petted."

Geyer had just enough time to get the safety off his 12 gauge shotgun and raise it to his shoulder when the Doberman lunged at him, teeth flashing.

"I let 'em have it with squirrel shot," he said. "It fell back, rolled over and staggered off into the shrubs again. They were still there...all of 'em, so I reloaded and got out of there."

As he hurried back to his truck, Geyer kept hearing the clanking of metal against metal.

"Dog tags," he told himself as he picked up the pace from a rush to a run. But the more he hurried, the louder the clanking became. Then he remembered the zippers on his flight boots.

"I was trying to escape from myself," he laughed as he concluded his tale.

Were it not for outdoorsmen like Geyer who share their adventures with a colorful, sometimes humorous touch, sports like hunting and fishing might never pass from one generation to the next. Were it not for colorful characters like Geyer on the Army Parachute Team, the Knights would not be nearly so "golden."

LEADERS' LEADERS

Almost every member of the Army Parachute Team is either a non-commissioned officer or officer, and therefore—a leader. Understanding this, the men and women who work in the Golden Knights' "head shed" can rightly be called "leaders' leaders."

The headquarters section is the largest part of the team, consisting of a command section, administrative section, operations, media relations, supply and the rigger loft.

Most of the members of headquarters are parachutists, many having even been through tryouts. Some of them, however, were specially selected to the team following a careful screening of their records, similar to the first step in bringing a prospective Knight to tryouts. They are then interviewed by both their section leader and the team first sergeant. If they're considered Golden Knight material, they're assigned to the team for a probationary period of not less than 90 days.

"We can't be hasty about bringing people onto this team," explained **First Sergeant Jeff Moon**. "We represent the entire Army, which means we want to ensure we get the best people in the Army, whether they're demonstrators, competitors, aviators or headquarters personnel."

Moon describes his own position as first sergeant as part psychiatrist/part chaplain and requiring a taste for blood "because you sometimes have to be able to fire somebody on the spot."

When asked if he ever had to fire anyone, Moon squints his eyes, producing an "are you serious?" expression.

"I've released my share," he answered. "You've got to remember, we don't use the UCMJ (Uniform Code of Military Justice) here on this team. We don't have to. No discipline problem ever gets that bad. If a member of this team does something foolish, he's simply telling his chain of command he no longer wants to be a member of this team. So, he's out of here."

Moon noted that writing a bad check or failing to pay your bills will get you in a lot of trouble in any unit, but on the Army Parachute Team, it will get you another assignment.

"Golden Knights represent the entire Army," he reiterated. "You have to keep that in mind all the time. We're in the public eye nearly every day. You can't have a good public image with problem people. You could say it's my job as first sergeant to protect our image by regulating who comes onto and who leaves this team."

Moon first enlisted in 1970 as a light weapons specialist with 1st Special Forces Group in Okinawa, then attended the HALO course in 1976 after reclassifying as a supply specialist. He served as team leader of the Geronimo Sport Parachute Team in Vicenza, Italy before coming to the Golden Knights as its supply sergeant in 1986. His promotion to E-8 in December 1987 resulted in his taking charge of the team as first sergeant.

With about 1,500 freefall parachute jumps to his credit, Moon not only runs the team as its senior NCO, he participates in numerous aerial demonstrations (60 shows in 1989 alone), and he serves as a judge for both Style & Accuracy and Relative Work at the U.S. Nationals. In recognition of his position and the job he's been doing, his subordinates and teammates elected him as the 1989 Golden Knight of the Year.

The team commander, **Lieutenant Colonel Kirk Knight**, took command in January 1989, continuing a tradition of commanders who began their military careers as enlisted soldiers. Knight is the team's 16th commander. His first encounter with the Golden Knights was with a former team member, **Lieutenant Danny Byard**, who was his platoon leader in Vietnam. Knight served a total of three tours in Vietnam, the first as an infantry paratrooper, the second as a Ranger and a third as a ''spotter'' plane pilot.

Knight attended OCS and flight school between his second and third tour in Vietnam. He was an infantry officer dually qualified as an aviator. When the Army finally made aviation a separate branch, he chose aviation.

Knight is a parachutist with nearly 3,000 jumps, an accelerated freefall instructor/examiner, and he's a pilot with over 3,000 flying hours. In fact, he's the only member of the team who can either jump at a demo, or fly for that demo. He sees his role as Commander to guide the team toward specific objectives, but allow his NCO's to run the team and bring his directives to fruition.

The other member of the command section, the executive officer, has the primary responsibility of procuring the personnel the first sergeant and/or the tryout cadre want to bring to the team. The job entails working closely with the branch managers of prospective team members—to get them assigned, or with Fort Bragg's Civilian Personnel Office—to fill civilian slots in aviation, supply, admin and media relations.

The current executive officer, **Captain** (promotable) **Paul Malone** is a parachutist and a West Point graduate, as was his predecessor, **Captain Marcus Bonds**. He's often the acting commander, as the team commander accompanies the competition team to nearly every major competition and the demonstration teams to special parachute demonstrations. But Malone's by no means a homebody or permanent rear detachment desk jockey. He also augments the demo teams. He also served as team leader during an international competition in Australia in November/December 1989.

Staff Sergeant Elizabeth Hunt, the administrative NCOIC, is perhaps the most unsung heroine on the team. She and **Sergeant Mike Scott**, the personnel staff and retention NCO, plus two civilian office assistants are as much responsible for keeping the team on the road as the aviation section is for keeping the team in the air. No administrative problem—leaves, pay discrepancies, reassignments—is ever left in an in-box unattended thanks to Hunt and her staff.

Sergeant First Class Mike Mayo runs the team rigger loft—a simple title, but a lot of responsibility. For, with the responsibility of ensuring proper packing and maintenance of parachutes, he is responsible for safety—

all aspects of safety, both in training, at competitions and during aerial demonstrations. He's also the head of the team's research and development segment. For his devotion to safety and tireless assistance to his teammates, Mayo was elected the 1987 Golden Knight of the Year.

Another former Golden Knight of the Year, **Chief Warrant Officer Four Fernando Musquiz**, is in charge of the team's supply section. He and his predecessor, **Chief Warrant Officer Three Jim New**, implemented several changes in the appearance of the supply section, namely the replacing of active duty positions with civilians. With a full-time budget analyst and supply clerk, they can control the team's millions of dollars in assets ranging from parachutes to aircraft to camera equipment and free up their active duty supply sergeant for other duties like traveling with the team to winter training.

Those who have led the Golden Knights as commanders, first sergeants or executive officers were painstakingly chosen by the Department of the Army. Just as Moon explained how important it is for the team to pick the right soldiers to the team, the Army is very discerning about who it picks to run its parachute team. The precedent to choose the best of the best was set by Brigadier General Stilwell, who hand-picked the men who were going to run the Army Parachute Team. Even today, they're hand-picked—but no longer by one general officer.

Over the years, those who have led the Golden Knights to their many achievements are many, some stronger than others, some remembered more than others. But none of the team's commanders or first sergeants were stronger or bettered remembered than the pair who started the team—**Jim Perry** and **John Hollis. Colonel Bruce Wicks** was com-

mander well after Perry, but one to be long remembered by his subordinates and teammates, as was his executive officer—**Captain Marcus Bonds. Master Sergeant** (retired) **Bobby "Spider" Wrenn** stands out in the team's long history as probably the most effective first sergeant since the original. All of these men had very different leadership styles and yet, all of them led the Golden Knights toward a golden future.

Captain (retired) Jim Perry, first Commander of the U.S. Army Parachute Team.

CAPTAIN (RETIRED) JAMES M. PERRY

He has a large-faced, battery-operated clock in every room of his home in Leroy, Alabama, and he changes the batteries for his clocks before they have a chance to run down.

"I have to know what time it is, all the time," explained Captain (retired) Jim Perry, first commander of the U.S. Army Parachute Team. "Time is important to me...always has been."

He was born February 24, 1927 in Tampa, Florida as James Madison Perry and began pushing the clock at an early age. By his 18th birthday, Perry was a private in the Marine Corps, taking part in the island by island assault leading up to the D-Day amphibious landing on Okinawa. After World War II, he served a year's occupation service in China. By 1949, he was a Marine sergeant stationed near Santa Anna, California and half-owner of a PT-17 war surplus plane purchased for a mere $800.

"As things happened at Orange (Airfield, now called 'John Wayne Airport'), two student pilots collided in mid-air, both wearing parachutes and neither jumped," he said. "I boasted that I'd be the first to jump, anything like that ever happened to me.

"'You're full of hot air, Perry,'" one of my buddies said. "'If we get the chutes, will you jump, just to show us you can?'"

The following week,

true to any worthwhile challenge, someone showed up with two old Switlicks, a 28-foot flat circular main with a 24-foot QAC for a reserve. And, of course, neither parachute was packed. Perry and his flying partner packed the chutes by following an instruction manual they'd borrowed from the packing section on the Marine base.

"I took the two rigs to 3,000 (feet) and did the first 1,000 foot tuck-and-tumble delay of my 3,000-plus jump career," he explained. "It was thrilling enough that when I landed, we re-packed and I went up for two more the same day."

Perry said afterwards they took the rigs to every California airshow they could go to. His partner flew the plane while Perry, the self-taught "skydiver," jumped, usually for $75 a jump. The two split the money after deducting for fuel cost. Sometimes they did as many as four shows a weekend.

"I was bringing home several hundred bucks

cash money every month," he said. "And that was when a sergeant made a total of $80 a month, rations included. I probably made 400 jumps then and was thinking about going deeper into Batwing jumps when the Korean War broke out, 25 June 1950."

Perry was deployed to Korea and took part in the Inchon Landing, the battle for Seoul and the Chosin Reservoir as an infantry platoon sergeant. At Chosin, 15,000 Marines were surrounded by 190,000 Chinese in one of the Corps' most glorious moments of battle.

Marine Colonel Raymond Murray was said to have responded to press questions about retreating, "We're coming out of here as Marines, or we're not coming out at all."

About half of them didn't come out, at least not alive. Those who did could say with pride they withstood not only overwhelming enemy forces, but the Korean winter pressing against them with temperatures of over 40 below zero, counting the wind chill factor. The few Marines who survived the Chosin Reservoir campaign call themselves the "Chosin Few."

As a result of the Korean Conflict and his leadership during it, Perry was commissioned as a second lieutenant in the Marine Corps, March 23, 1953, in armor now instead of infantry. He was promoted to first lieutenant 18 months later. He says he would have made captain in two more years, but got back into parachuting. At the time, the Marine Corps had no airborne units, nor any great use for parachuting, Perry explained. While he was jumping in Connecticut in 1956, he met Jacques Istel, who taught him the "French Cross" freefall position. This was his first formal training in the sport.

"I (later) met General James Gavin, who offered me a direct commission as a first lieutenant, same date of rank as my Marine commission, to come in the Army," Perry said. "He wanted me to teach stable-delay, he told me, 'because we're going to get into that business.' It would mean an automatic $110 pay raise for me—jump pay. I told the commandant of the Marine Corps the reason for my resignation and he let me go. So, I left the Marines with a Bronze Star and two Purple Hearts (Perry retired with a total of four Purple Hearts)."

Perry was commissioned as a signal officer effective January 3, 1958 and attended the signal officer's branch course at Fort Benning and Airborne School at Fort Bragg (even though he had 700 freefall jumps behind him). Gavin was true as his word and transferred Perry to 77th Special Forces Group. Following his Special Forces training in May 1959, he volunteered for Operation White Star and left for Laos for a year—one of the first 112 Special Forces (not yet Green Berets) troops to participate in that "covert, state-secret" operation.

He was promoted to captain in February 1960 and returned to Fort Bragg in May. It was upon his return that Brigadier General Stilwell called him into his office and announced his intentions for Perry's career and the course of military freefall parachuting.

"Joe (Stilwell) picked me, not for my parachuting experience, but because he needed a young captain—one not too ugly of face—with a little charisma—honey off his tongue sort of thing," Perry joked. He added seriously, "He also needed a combat officer he could keep home, not send off to Vietnam. I had enough ribbons to make that possible. Two wars and two Purple Hearts would keep me away from Vietnam as long as he wanted. Also, I had just returned from a 13-month tour in southeast Asia, a portion of that in combat."

Perry said Stilwell was close to every member of the team, like a father, in fact. In reverence to him, they even called him "Papa Joe," more often to his face than behind his back. Stilwell protected Perry from his enemies, who were mounting as the team grew. Many of those enemies, Perry believes, were not truly his own—running a parachute team wasn't that offensive to even its strongest opponents. He believes a lot of the hostility directed toward him was a way of getting to Stilwell who, Perry said, had "a lot" of enemies.

Perry's harassers referred to him as "Joe's Boy." Stilwell was apparently aware his enemies were sending unwarranted flack in Perry's direction in order to badger him, so he told "everyone" to keep their hands off Perry and his parachute team. Efforts to shut down the team failed even after the '61 Crash. The USAPT was firmly established and viable now. The need for a not-too-ugly captain—now a senior captain—with "the gift of gab," was no longer so great. Perry recognized it was time to move on.

Perry left the team to be airborne advisor to the Venezuelan Army, but his home was bombed there and his family threatened by terrorists. He was then transferred to the 8th Special Forces Group in Panama, commanded by Colonel "Bull" Simons, with whom Perry had served in Operation White Star in 1959. Simons, however, didn't welcome his old combat buddy aboard for he was in the process of locking horns with Stilwell, who was now assigned to the Special Forces Center back at Bragg. And Perry, after all, was still "Joe's Boy."

He volunteered several times to go to Vietnam, but Simons blocked his requests, even threatening his "existence" if he didn't settle down and be happy with an A-Team in Panama. After Perry was passed over for promotion to major, Stilwell rescued him and returned him to "The Hill" at Fort Bragg, this time as assistant training officer of Special Forces Training Group. In 1966 he was finally due for promotion to major and to be sent to Vietnam—finally—but as a "leg" infantry advisor. On May 31, 1966, Perry retired a very senior captain with 21 plus years service, 13 as a Marine and eight in the Army. His last assignment was as the HALO, SKYHOOK Committee chief for Special Forces Training Group.

"We were standing on the DZ one day, Joe (Stilwell) watching the rest of the team jump," Perry explained, grinning as he talked about the 'good old days.' "I smoked a lot in those days and he smoked not at all.

"This day he told me to quit smoking...and drinking too! I was putting away all I could hold then but never drunk on duty. He warned me there were those who had noticed and then said, 'You know, Jim, I'll never make major general and you'll never make major.' I've never told anyone but he added,

'but you stick with me and I'll see that you retire with honor.'"

Stilwell died in a plane crash in 1965 as a very senior brigadier general. Perry retired with honors as a very senior captain in 1966.

After retiring, Perry worked for the "state department" in the Mekong Delta. He lost his right hand in a rocket attack during the Tet Offensive in 1968, but resolved if he couldn't participate in a conflict, he'd report it. Besides, he'd been freelancing for newspapers and magazines since the late '50's. Perry wrote a screenplay called "China Rifles" in 1984, which remains on an option by Nexus Productions. In 1987 Perry was technical and script advisor on "Vietnam War Story" for HBO. At 58, he broke his leg while reporting on the Miskito Indian's Contra War with the Nicaraguans for SOLDIER OF FORTUNE and had to be secretly exfiltrated back into Honduras across the jungled river frontier.

"I was shooting pic-

tures of some Indian refugees...women and children, mostly...when I stepped to one side, looking through the camera instead of where I was standing," he explained. "Next thing I knew I was at the bottom of a muddy river bank with my leg busted. There wasn't a medic there, so I had to set it myself by wedging my foot in the fork of two small trees and twisting. I was still wearing a cast a couple months later when I was covering the 1985 elections in El Salvador."

Perry is currently working on three separate novels, "Millions to Burn" (which takes place in Laos), "Out Past the Wire (which takes place in the Central Highlands of Vietnam) and "Roggo," a five book series that tells the story of an aging Green Beret who can't stay away from adventure. Just how much of his books are fiction and how much memories, only Perry knows, although the first book has Roggo "stomping around" in the Rio Coco country of Honduras along the Nicaraguan border.

Without a doubt, Perry is a story within a story, a book waiting to be written. But he'll modestly say as he shakes his head, "Don't waste white space on me. There are too many other colorful characters on the Team."

During the 1989 Golden Knight Alumni Association Reunion, Perry attended for the very first time. Team members past and present lined up to meet the first commander, the man responsible for making their Team a team.

"Captain," **Sergeant First Class Bill Yeider** said respectfully as he sat down beside Perry and introduced himself. "I'd like to ask you a question."

"Go ahead, Son," Perry told him. He addressed nearly every one of the more than 400 team members attending "son" or "young lady."

"Sir," Yeider continued, waving his hand and gesturing toward the mass of people crowded in the huge banquet hall, "did you ever expect this thing... this team to get this big?"

"No," he answered, smiling. "No. I didn't. I always figured sooner or later someone would find out we were just jumping out of airplanes, which is what we wanted to do anyway, and that the Army was paying us to do it. At best, I figured we had five or six years."

The Golden Knights started their 1990 show and competition season in early March with some anticipation for the nine months ahead of them. But few team members watch the calendar the way Perry watches the clock. He's the father of six children—three boys and three girls. Perry is a man who knows full well there's a time for everything—a time to begin and a time to end. But he and the men and women he has inspired, hope and pray the clock keeps on ticking for his Army Parachute Team.

Although he had a "couple hundred" delayed fall jumps (700 in fact) when he left the Marine Corps and accepted an Army commission, Perry had to go to Airborne School. This photo was of his graduation in 1958.

Command Sergeant Major (retired) John Hollis, first First Sergeant of the U.S. Army Parachute Team.

COMMAND SERGEANT MAJOR (RETIRED) JOHN HOLLIS

John Hollis was called "First Soldier" by his commander, Jim Perry—a fitting title for the senior NCO on a team of NCO's. But even before he became first sergeant of the Army Parachute Team, Hollis had made up his mind to be a professional soldier.

"I worked my way up to command sergeant major," he said, emphasizing the word *worked*. "Of course, that's when things start to get easier. You work for just one man instead of a whole bunch of 'em."

Hollis enlisted in April 1945, in time to see action on various Japanese islands before the A-bomb was dropped, ending World War II. Following the war, he remained stationed in Yanome, Japan, and earned his jump wings with the 11th Airborne Division—later serving as an airborne instructor there and with the 8th Army's Air Transportability School.

He was still stationed in Japan in 1950 when the Korean War broke out. During that conflict, he took part in the first aerial resupply drops. His unit was responsible for dropping a badly needed bridge into the Chosin Reservoir where 15,000 Marines—including one who would be his commander in ten years time, were both impressed and quite ap-preciative of their airdrop.

Following the Korean War, Hollis was assigned to the Army's Mountain and Cold Weather Training Command at Fort Carson, Colorado. His next assignment was the 77th Special Forces at Fort Bragg, where he underwent Special Forces training and delayed-fall training. In September 1959, he was picked by Major Merrill Sheppard to be the NCOIC of the STRAC Sport Parachute Team—a position later to be that of first sergeant when the team became a unit. In any case, he held that position through all the name changes for three and a half years.

"One man was really responsible for keeping the team from falling apart after the crash in '61," Jim Perry reminded his teammates at the 1989 reunion dinner. "John Hollis broke his back in that crash and could have stayed home on quarters, but no, he came in to work. He ran the team...everything... so those of us not hurt in that crash could meet demands on the team for demos and competitions. Hollis kept this team together."

The authority delegated to Hollis by Perry remained the prerogative of Golden Knight first sergeants to follow, despite efforts to change things back to the way officers ran most units, where the commander micromanaged every aspect of the unit. Perry's successor tried to re-assert some of the authority that he thought was rightfully his as commander.

"If Joe Norman or Squeaky Charette came to me and said, 'Top, I got all my stuff packed up to leave tomorrow. I need to run downtown.' And I'd say, 'Sure. Take off.' Roy (Martin) didn't like that. But I told him, 'Roy, you don't have time for that. That's my job to authorize people to go to town.'"

Hollis says he and Roy Martin came to an understanding that they were not going to be able to work together because Martin believed Hollis had too much power as first sergeant. And since he had no intention of giving up, or giving back such power, Hollis asked for a 3-day pass to visit the Department of the Army and obtain a new assignment. He returned with orders for the 7th Infantry Division in Korea. Martin told him he'd never make it with a by-the-rules unit, so he was more than a little surprised when Hollis returned from Korea as an E-9.

Hollis was assigned as operations sergeant in the S-3 Special Troops section in April 1963. The greatest part of his job was monitoring all parachuting activities in South Korea. He was promoted to sergeant major and returned to Fort Bragg as a command sergeant major in the 2nd Battalion, 508th Infantry of the 82d Airborne Division. A year following his return to the states, his unit was deployed to the Dominican Republic for 17 months. While they were there, the Golden Knights came to perform for the morale of the troops, and to show the American flag.

In 1969 Hollis received orders for his fourth armed conflict—this time, Vietnam. He served as command sergeant major of the 2nd Battalion, 173rd Airborne Brigade. He retired shortly after he returned from Vietnam in 1971 with more than 25 years service and more than 1000 parachute jumps.

"I retired and took a year off," he said, grinning. "I did everything around the house that needed doing, then I got a job."

Hollis found work in a local convenience store as a stockroom clerk-cashier. As he had done when he started his military career, he worked his way up and is now a district supervisor for that store chain. At the same reunion dinner in which he was so recognized by his former commander, Hollis—the "First Soldier," spoke to his troops.

"You just keep getting better and better," he

told them. "And I just want you to know, I'm mighty proud of you."

Coming from the team's First Soldier, that was quite a compliment.

Colonel Bruce Wicks, former team commander.

COLONEL BRUCE WICKS

"Well, hey, Big Guy!" he says whenever he greets a former teammate. This greeting is followed by a firm handshake and an effervescent grin.

Such is the down-home nature of Colonel Bruce Wicks, a West Chester, Pennsylvania native and commander of the Golden Knights from May 1987 to January 1989. His selection as commander was the most logical choice, for Wicks has had a long history with parachuting, having made nearly 2,500 freefall parachute jumps.

After graduating from West Chester High School in 1960, he completed his bachelor's in physical education at Lock Haven State University in 1964, then enlisted as an infantry paratrooper. Just prior to airborne school, he married his high school sweetheart, Kay Huey. They now have two children, Robin and Rocky.

Wicks left the enlisted ranks little more than a year after he joined the Army by graduating from OCS. He then went on to Special Forces training and two tours in Vietnam. After attending the HALO course in 1969, he put aside his static line in favor of freefall parachuting.

Since that year, Wicks has completed his master's in physical education at the University of Illinois, and he served as deputy commander of the physical education department at West Point, as well as deputy commander of 7th Special Forces Group.

But when he became commander of the Golden Knights, Wicks says he obtained the best job in the Army. He worked diligently to promote both the Army and the sport of parachuting. The Knights' participation in the 1988 Summer Olympics was the capstone of his efforts, he said.

"I think we made a giant step," he said, enthusiastically. "Our parachute exhibition went over flawlessly. I think we really rolled their socks down!"

Wicks says the Olympic stadium was packed with more than 100,000 people who all began screaming as over 80 parachutists flew into the stadium. The exhibition itself consisted of three aircraft in trail.

The first plane deposited 22 R.O.K. (Republic of Korea) Special Forces soldiers into the cheering crowd. The second plane carried the national champions of 22 countries, including Golden Knights **Chuck Lackey** and **Bob Finn**.

The trailing aircraft carried the main event, the Olympic rings' jumpers. All of these participants were either current or former relative work world champions. Six Golden Knights dressed in (appropriately enough) gold jump suits made up the lower left ring. They included **Glenn Bangs, Chris Wagner, Andy Gerber, Jim Coffman, Charley Brown** and **Willie Lee**. A 10th Golden Knight, **Paul Rafferty**, remained on the ground as an alternate, while Wicks coordinated the jump through his role on the opening ceremonies' organization committee.

"My job was to put it all together," Wicks explained. "We practiced for a week in Davis, California just in case the weather prevented us from practicing when we got to Seoul. During one of the rehearsals there at Seoul, I sat with President Parks, who was the president of SL.O.O.C. (Seoul Olympic Organization Committee)."

Parks was so impressed with their parachute exhibition, he invited all the parachutists to have lunch with him to express his appreciation for their tremendous performance. Wicks couldn't disagree with his assessment, noting theirs was indeed a tough act to follow.

"I've been on numerous U.S. National Parachute teams," Wicks said. "In 1988 I also served as team leader of the U.S. Style & Accuracy Parachute Team in Sweden. But this was a thrill that will be long remembered."

Wicks was a commander long to be remembered. Even though he was "a full bird colonel," explained **Bill Jackson**, Wicks was the kind of commander who didn't need an "open door policy," for it was common knowledge that he was available to his subordinates at any time for advice, assistance or just plain conversation.

Wicks left the Army Parachute Team in January 1989 for an assignment with the Special Operations Command in Panama. He was deputy commander for operations in Panama City, December 18, 1989, when combined forces from Panama and the U.S. ended the dictatorship of General Manuel Noriega.

He says he'll always be proud of having commanded the Golden Knights. "Men and women," he says, "who represent the kind of professional, dedicated soldiers who helped rid the world of a dictator and drug dealer." Wicks' next assignment will be at Fort Benjamin Harrison, Indiana as director of the Army's physical fitness center. Despite this non-airborne assignment, he'll still be an avid parachutist.

"I'll always be

involved in parachuting," he said. "It's one of the loves of my life. I may not be assigned to the Golden Knights anymore, but I'll always be a Golden Knight. I'll support this team and these guys who supported me in whatever way I can."

The Golden Knight Alumni Association has a slogan, "Once a Knight, always a Knight." Bruce Wicks epitomizes that slogan.

Captain Marcus Bonds, former team executive officer.

CAPTAIN MARCUS BONDS

He could have stayed home in Paterson, New Jersy and joined the OPFOR (opposing forces)— street gangs who push drugs, rob and assault the American public. But Captain Marcus Bonds chose to join an honorable organization. He decided to be a soldier.

In June 1979 Bonds graduated from the U.S. Army Military Academy at West Point, New York. His greatest military achievement to date, he believes, was serving as executive officer—second in command—of the U.S. Army Parachute Team.

"If I hadn't gone to college, I might be in jail or dead by now," Bonds explained.

He pointed out that many of his high school classmates were now in one of those two categories. Bonds attributes his decision to escape the same fate to his physical education teacher—a retired Air Force lieutenant colonel, who impressed upon him the benefits of a military education and career.

"I'd been offered a football scholarship by Hope College in Michigan," Bonds said. "But my P.E. instructor, Mr. Graham...I don't remember his first name. Anyway, he got me interested in the Air Force Academy."

Bonds says he listened to his instructor because he respected his opinion, but also because the thought of flying F-4

Phantom jets awakened a spirit of adventure he never thought existed in him. He wanted to be a pilot.

His application process included a civilian screening board whose members asked him why he wanted to go to the Air Force Academy. His answer was simply that he wanted to fly. Not having come from a military family or even having known anyone else in the military, he was surprised when the board recommended him for both the Air Force Academy and West Point.

A physical exam revealed that his depth perception was less than the required perfect vision to fly Phantoms, so he made a last minute decision to go to West Point. But flying aircraft was not the only kind of flying he had an interest in.

"West Point has its own sport parachute team," Bonds said, grinning like a kid caught with his hand in the cookie jar. "They're called the 'Black Knights.'"

Bonds says that only five percent of his West Point class was black and an even smaller percentage of the Black Knights were, in fact, black. But he wanted to try parachuting for the experience—for the thrill. And the thrill was greater than he anticipated. He loved it. That love for the sport would later induce a concentrated effort to become a part of the most famous parachute team in the world. In August 1986 Bonds was assigned to the Golden Knights as its operations officer. About a year later, he became the executive officer.

Only a year before coming to the Army Parachute Team, Bonds had changed his branch from infantry to aviation, finally realizing his dream of becoming a pilot. Previous experience as a staff officer, however, "pegged" him as someone capable of cutting through red tape and getting the personnel and logistical support his unit needed.

"I had been assigned as the Battalion S-3 (training section leader) as a second lieutenant right after I finished my infantry training," he explained. "After flight school, my first assignment was also a staff job. I was the only captain in the Army to work as the primary G-3 Air (division level aviation coordinator). This was a major's position."

As a Golden Knight, Bonds refused to be tied down by his "staff" reputation. Whenever an opportunity presented itself, he volunteered to "go on the road" with one of the demonstration teams. In fact, during his last three months on the team, he traveled nearly every weekend with the Black Team. He grins broadly when asked why he chose the Black Team.

"You've got to understand," he explained, waving his hands in the air with one of those Baptist minister-type gestures. "Parachuting is still not that popular among blacks, mostly because so few blacks are exposed to the sport."

Although several black soldiers are currently on the Army Parachute Team, only one is a parachute demonstrator. Bonds says that number simply reflects the limited number of blacks in the Army who skydive, either through the Army's HALO course, or sport parachute clubs. He notes that the same problem exists with few women jumpers. He emphasizes that the Army is the most equal opportunity employer in the country—minorities have filled the pages of team history from the beginning.

A team leader and an assistant team leader currently on the team are Hispanic. Blacks too have held prominent positions on the team. **Sergeant First Class Alsee Richardson**, now a retired sergeant major, was a team leader, and **Staff Sergeant Cecil Davis** was a member of the Gold Team killed in the '73 Crash.

Bonds says he dedicated a great deal of his time on the road with the demo teams to changing perceptions about the sport among young blacks.

"Parachuting is a sport for all Americans," he said.

Few inter-city kids get an opportunity to even meet a soldier, let alone a Golden Knight, Bonds says. Perhaps that's why so many looked up to Bonds as a black role model when he traveled with the team. Most children and many adults might have some difficulty in defining gallantry, but nearly everyone can recognize it when they see it.

Like so many symbols which have been redefined over the centuries, the image of the "black knight" in fables and legends has gone from malicious, to mysterious, to magnanimous. Bonds likes the current image. Since leaving the team for a new assignment as an ROTC instructor—a man responsible for turning out a new generation of leaders—the image fits him. Black Knight or Golden Knight, Bonds can be "pegged" as a knight indeed.

Master Sergeant (retired) Bobby "Spider" Wrenn, former team first sergeant and 1969 Golden Knight of the Year.

MASTER SERGEANT (RETIRED) BOBBY WRENN

A sign above the first sergeant's door used to read, "Spider's Web, Crawl In." Inside his office, Bobby "Spider" Wrenn kept yet another sign, this one more serious: "Your laurels are known to many, but the toil, dedication and sacrifice are known only to those who've given." He should know for he

202

gave the Army nearly 30 years service, from the day he received his draft notice in 1952, to the day he retired in 1981 as first sergeant of the Golden Knights.

Wrenn actually served two tours with the team, from 1966 to 1969 as a parachute demonstrator, operations NCOIC and IO director, and from 1977 to 1981 as first sergeant. He made his first parachute jump in 1956 at Airborne School. Four years later he witnessed the Golden Knights jump and rushed right over to the XVIII Airborne Corps Sport Parachute Club to sign up for freefall classes. Two years later, he was running that club.

Sometime between his becoming president of the Corps Club and becoming a Golden Knight (he doesn't recall the exact date), Wrenn had the silhouette of a spider sewn on the inside of his parachute canopy. Thereafter, he became known around the drop zones and parachute clubs as "Spider." To this day

the nickname has stuck with him. Little did his comrades know he had acquired the name "Spider" years before while attending Fayetteville Senior High School.

"A cheerleader made the comment that I had more arms and legs than a spider," he said. "The name 'Spider' just sort of stuck with me after that."

Wrenn made use of his long arms, at least, by becoming a drummer. Despite growing up at Fort Bragg and witnessing airborne operations on an almost daily basis, he had little inclination to jump out of airplanes. His only interest was music. But when he was 22 and his drumming career was about to take off, he got his draft notice. A few short months later, following basic training, he was again beating the drums, this time as part of the 307th Army Band at Fort McClellan, Alabama.

"That's where all the WAC's (Women's Army Corps) were back then," he interjected, grinning from ear to

ear.

He won an all-Army talent contest, then went on to play on the Ed Sullivan Show, a popular television show of the '50's and '60's which hosted such talents as Elvis Presley and the Beatles. His apparent success as a drummer made him feel all the more like "a typical draftee," Wrenn said. He had grown up the son of an Army master sergeant at the Home of the Airborne, but he wanted nothing to do with the Army. He only wanted to do his time and get back to civilian music. He did, but a short 89 "lean" days later, Wrenn was back in uniform, this time to stay.

Except for a one year tour with the 101st Airborne Division in Vietnam in 1969-70, Wrenn would spend the rest of his military career at Fort Bragg.

"There's not a lot of airborne snare drummers in the Army," he chuckled. "That's how I got to stay at Fort Bragg so long. But I didn't mind. This is home to me, anyway.''

Wrenn came to the team as a demonstrator on the Gold Team, then went to operations a year later. The team was in Zephyrhills, Florida in 1968 to attack world records. His job was to record those records as the FAI (Federation Aeronautique Internationale) representative. The crash in which he and other team members were involved caused some problems for those records attempts. Not only was the team short at least two members, Wrenn had to be there or the record jumps could not be counted as official. Despite a broken leg, two broken ribs, two cracked vertebrae and multiple lacerations, Wrenn climbed out of his hospital bed to lay on the drop zone and record his teammates' record attempts.

The dedication he displayed eventually resulted in his teammates electing him as their 1969 Golden Knight of the Year. That distinction and his earned

reputation as president of the 82d Sport Parachute Club—which he became after he came back from Vietnam, led to his returning to the team in 1977 as its first sergeant. As the ''Top Knight,'' Wrenn reminded his subordinates and teammates every day the opportunities they had were earned by each team member one day at a time. Being a Golden Knight was not simply a matter of jumping out of planes or wearing a black and gold uniform.

''There's no school anywhere in the world, no Army manual, no SQT (Skill Qualification Test) that can make a Golden Knight,'' he told them in a private ceremony honoring his retirement. ''Dedication is what makes you unique.''

In his 20-year association with sport parachuting, Wrenn is credited with training over 7,000 soldiers in freefall parachuting. Shortly after retiring from the team, he took up the permanent position as secretary/treasurer of

the Golden Knight Alumni Association. His ever-friendly face is the first one former team members are greeted by each year at the annual reunion. According to **Andy Gerber**, who organized the 1988 and 1989 reunions, more than anyone else in the association—past or present members of the team, the success of the reunions can be attributed directly to Wrenn. With everything he does, he dedicates himself completely.

Aside from placing funny signs over his door, or thought-provoking signs on his office wall, Wrenn is credited with coining a closing statement to team aerial demonstrations still used by narrators today.

''May all your days be prosperous and all your 'Knights' golden,'' Wrenn told a young lady, Carol Chase, after autographing a team photograph for her. To this day, Ms. Chase says she still has that picture.

Wrenn's military career was long and diverse, going from

draftee to retiree, from making music to judging world parachuting records. And yet, each Golden Knight travels to the beat of a different drum. The drums may be different, but the beat is the same. The dedication Wrenn talked about on the day he retired, is the beat that sets the tempo for the Army Parachute Team. Current and future team members will be ever-grateful to men like Spider Wrenn for showing them how to play it.

EVERY DAY HEROES

The man was choking, grabbing his throat with both hands, coughing as he doubled over. His faced reddened and his eyes watered from the piece of chicken blocking his wind pipe. Many of the people around the banquet table sat there aghast. A few came over and hit him on the back, trying to dislodge whatever was choking him. Most just called for help, for someone to do some-thing. **Staff Sergeant Jason Davis** did something.

Davis approached the man from behind, wrapped his arms around him, cupping his fists under the man's chest. One good inward thrust and the chicken came up. The man could breathe. Davis disappeared into the crowd attracted by all the attention. He left before the man or any one else could identify, or have the chance to thank him.

Cleveland, September 1989.

It took some investigation, but not very much. After all, all the Golden Knights attending the social engagement following the day's airshow were in the same uniform, gray slacks and blue pullover shirts. Davis was discovered sitting among his teammates and thanked properly for saving a man's life with the Heimlich Maneuver. He was quick to react when the man needed help, but reluctant to accept praise for "doing what anybody else would have done."

Davis is not an Army medic or civilian EMT (Emergency Medical Technician). He's just a soldier with basic first aid training and a willingness to help others calmly and confidently, without expectation of reward or gratitude. He is, quite simply, a Golden Knight—your average, every day hero.

Baton Pass

Two jumpers glide together in free fall and pass a baton from one jumper to the other.

They separate, deploy their parachutes and land on target.

Cutaway

A jumper deliberately causes his parachute to collapse, releases it and returns to free fall.

Then he deploys his second parachute.

Diamond Track

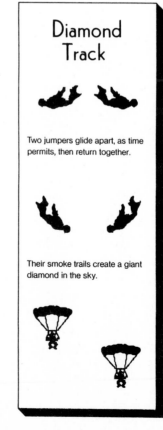

Two jumpers glide apart, as time permits, then return together.

Their smoke trails create a giant diamond in the sky.

Diamond Formation

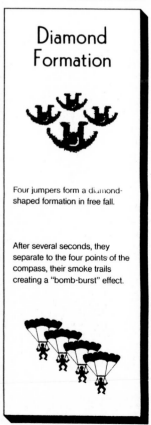

Four jumpers form a diamond-shaped formation in free fall.

After several seconds, they separate to the four points of the compass, their smoke trails creating a "bomb-burst" effect.

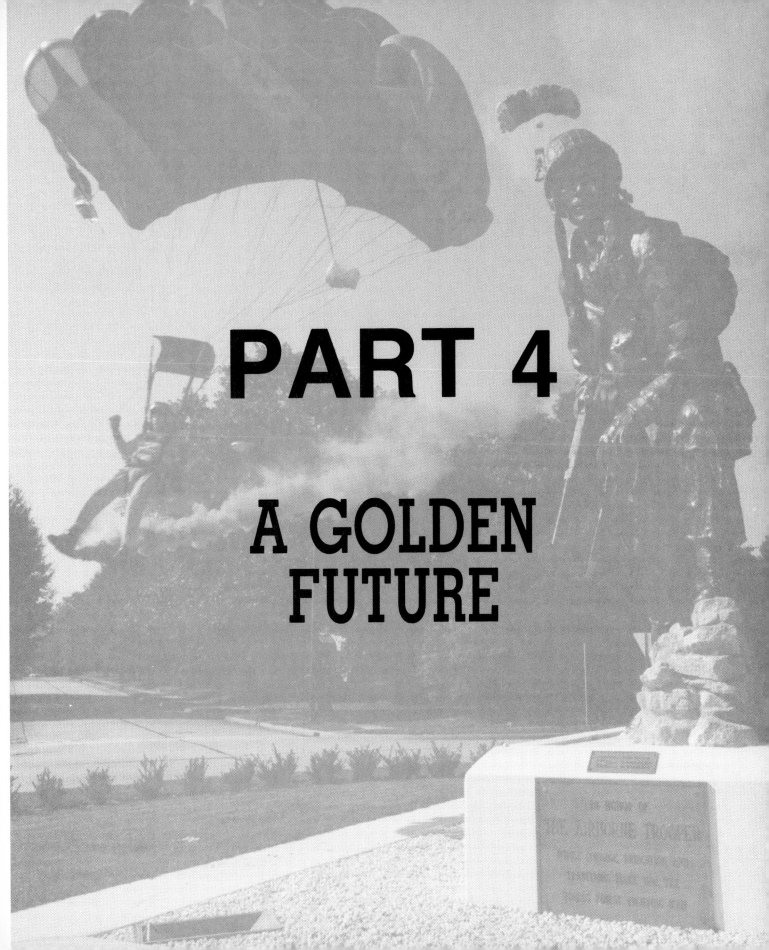

PART 4

A GOLDEN FUTURE

PART 4

A GOLDEN FUTURE

GOLDEN KNIGHT 2000

There's a term being thrown about in team headquarters and the Department of the Army which represents a list of desired goals and changes for the U.S. Army Parachute Team to be accomplished by the end of this decade. That term is "Golden Knight 2000." The list, according to **Major Paul Malone**, the team executive officer, includes both a lot of wishful thinking for monies and assets probably never to be realized, and serious plans to make changes to the team—changes that will enhance the team's ability to promote the Army, compete in national and international parachute competitions and research and develop parachuting techniques and equipment.

"The consensus among team leaders is an overall need for more money," Malone said. "But the team's budget is currently frozen at $2 million a year. More than half of that goes toward spare parts and maintenance of our four airplanes, two of which we want to replace as soon as possible."

One unrealistic suggestion regarding money, Malone says, was that the team's budget should be "fenced." That is, whenever the Defense Department was forced to make budget cuts, its demonstration teams should be protected as too valuable a recruiting asset to be slighted a single dollar. If the Strategic Defense Initiative ("Star Wars") couldn't be fenced or designated as "hands off" to Congressional budget cutters, there was no reason to expect the Army Parachute Team or any of the DoD demo teams would be so privileged.

Several suggestions for improving public relations involved legal risks no one would seriously want to support, he added. For example, as the team has several "tandem masters," it seemed like a good idea for Golden Knights to give tandem jumps for VIP's before special shows. A tandem jump requires a larger than normal parachute and a special jump harness built for two. The tandem master, who appears to be riding his student "piggyback," controls the parachute, but the student is still able to experience the feeling of freefalling. The legal risks are obvious. As **Sergeant First Class Mike Mayo**, the team's safety officer, explains, "one tandem parachuting accident and the team's reputation would be ruined."

"Tandem jumps are for people genuinely interested in the sport, but (who) aren't sure they want to invest time and money into something they might not enjoy," Mayo said. "They're not for joy riders and shouldn't be used as a publicity gimmick."

Another less controversial suggestion to extend the same courtesy (of accompanying the team on their lifts) to local politicians and celebrities currently allowed the media was not as black and white as hoping to fence the budget, says Malone. The Army has regulations which allow the press to ride military aircraft, but few provisions for extending that invitation to anyone else. Given the special mission of the Army Parachute Team to promote the Army, an exception would seem possible. As executive officer, obtaining such an exception for the Knights now falls on Malone.

Pro Pay (special allowances given to soldiers performing duties deemed essential by the Army) is another item of interest to team members being placed on Malone. Already, he was tasked with securing HALO pay for team members in addition to the regular jump pay awarded to all airborne soldiers. These special pay incentives are intended to attract and maintain quality soldiers in high risk jobs. Malone believes he can best accomplish this goal for the team by earning recognition of a special MOS (Military Occupational Specialty) for members of the Army

Parachute Team. The MOS would qualify team members for special pay incentives and alleviate another "irritant"—SQT.

The annual SQT (Skill Qualification Test) can become an annual hassle for team members with highly technical MOS's such as signal or special operations. Testing of these job skills is difficult enough without that soldier being separated from his normal duties for years at a time while serving on the Army Parachute Team. If Golden Knights were awarded a special MOS, their annual tests would be controlled locally, which would alleviate the additional problem of bringing Golden Knights off the road to take SQT's during the times scheduled by the Department of the Army. All Golden Knights could then be tested at one time, most likely at the end of the demonstration/competition season.

If such an MOS was awarded, a request for increased stabilization of team members would be on its heels. Currently,

Golden Knights serve a 3-year tour. Team leaders argue that increasing the stabilization period to six years would decrease personnel turnovers, which would increase the level of experience on both the demo and comp teams. The demo teams see this increased experience as a decrease in the number of injuries, as most injuries such as torn knee ligaments are incurred by new team members. The comp teams would benefit most, not only by decreased injuries, but their level of competitiveness would be increased dramatically.

Following the 1989 world championships, for example, nearly half of the Knights' Relative Work Team—the world champions—were lost to reassignments. The team is now tasked to rebuilding itself in time to defend its world title in 1991, a task normally requiring twice that many competition seasons. But increasing stabilization would only partially prevent this comp team slaughter from re-occurring.

When the team was officially established in 1961, its mission statement officially said the Army Parachute Team was formed to provide "a pool" of highly skilled freefall parachutists who would promote the Army through aerial demonstrations, "participate" in national and international parachute competitions and conduct research and development on the military aspects of freefall parachuting. That mission statement said nothing about demonstration and competition teams, nor did it say the team was to do everything within the resources available to it to win parachute competitions.

The most important and perhaps most challenging goal for the Army Parachute Team is to re-write its own mission statement. Such a re-writing would require approval comparable to the steps early team members undertook to get the team official recognition. But if the mission statement is re-written, says Malone, it will not be a drastic revision, but the removal of at least two hurdles. Instead of "a pool" of highly skilled freefall parachutists, the mission statement would be changed to include "specified teams" (demonstration and competition). Such wording could justify enlargements of existing teams, or the addition of other demo or comp teams.

The key words needing re-structuring in the mission statement would involve changing "participate" in national and international parachute competition to "organize competition teams and win." Although the Golden Knights have had a tremendous history of successes in parachute competitions, its successes have been sporadic during the world championships— the competition which means the most to parachutists around the world, and, therefore, the one most countries devote most of their energies and assets. By recognizing "winning" as part of the team's mission, the Golden Knights could perhaps defer critical reassignments and justify additional training support.

The aviation section envisions a larger fleet of quality aircraft and twice the number of pilots. With the suggestion of an additional demonstration team, for example, the aviators counter with the supporting costs of another plane and more pilots to get that team around the country. In the headquarters, both operations and media relations note the extra team will require at least one additional person in each office to support that team. Likewise, a call for another competition team receives the same response from aviation and headquarters. The costs, therefore, are not limited to simply added personnel and the parachutes they'd need to perform or compete.

However, additions are in the making. Since **Cheryl Stearns** and

Terry Bennett Vares left the team in the mid-'80's, the Knights have not had a world champion woman competitor. An all-women Style & Accuracy Team is at the top of the wish list for team additions. But as Malone explains, that goal is still a ways off, not only because of the logistic cost of supporting a new team, but due to the limited number of women soldiers who try out for the team each year.

"I want to see more women on this team," **Lieutenant Colonel Kirk Knight** told his team leaders. "Get the word out to the parachute clubs. If you find a woman who's interested in becoming a Golden Knight, but not quite up to par as a jumper, I expect you as NCO's and as Golden Knights to encourage, guide, and, well, tutor her along if you have to. We can't get more women on the team if they don't come to tryouts. And we can't get them to tryouts unless we let them know there's a place for them on this team."

Knight paused to emphasize he wasn't suggesting to tryout cadre that team standards should be changed in order for women to "pass" tryouts. There's only one standard on the Golden Knights and that's "the best of the best." A separate all-women competition team might one day be a reality, but each member of that team would first have to have meet the prerequisites of being Golden Knights.

Another competition team, one for Canopy Relative Work (CRW), is also in the planning stages and one that may be implemented by the end of the 1990 season. In fact, the Knights entered a CRW event during the 1989 Australian Military Nationals and walked away with the top three team places. "The talent," says Malone, who was part of the third place team in that competition, "is already there." But given the personnel losses the Relative Work Team suffered at the end of 1989, the people needed to make up a

4-man CRW Team would have to come from the demo teams until such a team was authorized by the Table of Organization & Equipment (TO&E). If a shortage on one of the demo teams occurred, these jumpers would immediately be recalled, thus shutting down the newly formed CRW Team until the emergency passed. This "start'n stop" scenario is highly disfavored by both demonstration team leaders and the prospective members of the planned CRW Team.

Malone noted that several items on his "Golden Knight 2000" report included the testing and buying of replacements for the team's two U21's, used primarily for training by the competition teams. Another not-too-distant change also involves the aviation section—maintenance and hanger facilities exclusively for the Golden Knights. Plans are in still in the approval stages to move the aviators to Pope Air Force Base from Simmons Army Airfield. As those facilities are not yet built, Malone points out that he won't be seeing those plans come to fruition, but hopefully his successor will.

It has also been argued that the U.S. Army Parachute Team should be moved from the Home of the Airborne, Fort Bragg, North Carolina, to some location central to the United States such as Oklahoma, where the U.S. Nationals were held from 1981 to 1990. A centralized location would save on the fuel cost of flying from North Carolina to, say, Colorado, and return, only to fly back to Arizona the following weekend. Malone sees little chance of such a move, however, citing both the costs of the move and the break with the team's heritage. The Army Parachute Team, afterall, represents the epitome of the airborne. Moving the team from its birthplace and home is simply unthinkable to most.

PERSONAL GOALS

Each team and each member of them has personal goals which they consider as either needed or nice to have for improving the overall image of "The Team." The demonstration teams, for example, want to do more special event shows like the performance for President George Bush at his inauguration. In support of the demo teams, the media relations office has suggested "The Team" now do a special aerial demonstration for the Panamanian people and U.S. troops assigned in Panama. After all, The Team did such a show following the Grenada Invasion in 1983 and in the Dominican Republic in 1965.

The aviation section has suggested with some emphasis the team's F27 Fokker (now redesignated C-31) is fully capable of overseas travel and should be considered for use in European tours. Of course, there's no argument from the demo teams here. Show schedules, however, are decided months before the start of a show season and "add-ons" are difficult to get in, given the Knights' overall mission to support Army recruiting— something a European tour would not do.

One special show scheduled for the 1990 season is participation in the celebration of the 50th anniversary of the airborne—a celebration taking place in Washington, D.C. in July 1990. While the team is there, the media relations office again has PR plans in the works, this time for a photo mission whereby a Golden Knight would land near the Vietnam Memorial trailing the MIA/POW flag from his suspension lines. The photo would be used to arouse America's conscience that the war will never be over until all those who fought it are accounted for.

Permeating the personal wish list are suggestions from the team's media relations office that they could use additional personnel to promote the team's image. Among those suggestions, the "image makers" recommend the team be placed under the direction of the Department of the Army Public Affairs Office instead of U.S. Army Recruiting through Forces Command. The continued support of the U.S. Army Parachute Team is dependent on the publicity it gains for the Army. And genuine publicity consists of more than a good advertising campaign.

The competition teams look toward an Olympic future, but one obviously distant—at least until parachuting is seen as a viable commercial sport. The first step toward reaching that goal, however, would require parachuting itself to be recognized and treated as a genuine sport by the news media. Sometime between then and now, the Knights' competitors envision an Olympic-style training center for use not only by the Army Parachute Team, but also as an Olympic training site of all parachuting competitors. Since the Golden Knights are recognized and requested world-wide for competition seminars, such a training center run by the Golden Knights would only increase their reputation as trainers of the sport they master.

The competitors also desire a physician and perhaps even a psychiatrist attached to the team. Simple injuries like a pulled muscle or twisted ankle cannot be allowed to keep a competitor down. Currently, team members are able to look out for each other to a limited degree with the aid of Army medical specialist within the team. A more permanent, more expert solution is preferable, though. Then there's the "attitude thing," the "can I really beat that guy?" syndrome which can preoccupy the competitor's mind and sometimes prevent him from giving 100 percent to his event.

"Every major professional football team in the country has a shrink working for them," explained **Sergeant First Class Gary Mohler**, team leader of the Style & Accuracy Team. "Well, we're professionals, too, and I think attaching a psychiatrist to the team for competitions is something we should look into."

The man who describes his job as being "part shrink," First **Sergeant Jeff Moon**, is looking for his own replacement. Moon will leave the team in the summer of 1990 to attend the Sergeants Major Academy. His job as first sergeant of the team was raised to an E-9 position in 1988, thus allowing for the most senior NCO to run the Army's team of NCO's. Moon's concern about who will replace him is the same concern he has for taking anyone on the team, only greater. His replacement, he feels, must be a senior E-8 or E-9 who is an experienced freefall parachutist. If he's not a parachutist, Moon doesn't believe he'll have the working knowledge to run a team of parachutists, and not just any parachutists, but the best parachutists in the world.

"If he's not a freefall parachutist, he won't know what's going on," Moon explained. "That means he can mess everything up trying to run this team like some ordinary unit, or he'll spend so much time trying to figure out what's going on, he won't get anything done."

As would be expected, the current commander, **Lieutenant Colonel Kirk Knight**, has goals of his own for the team. His priority is replacing the team's U21's, an indication that Knight is an aviator who understands the importance of providing the best aviation support with dependable aircraft. Knight also intends to continue to carry the Olympic torch lit years ago. Following the 1989 world championships in Spain, it was determined that another parachute exhibition would be in order for the 1992 Olympics, but the Olympics were still

not ready for parachuting as an event. Nonetheless, he will help coordinate the team's involvement in the '92 opening ceremonies.

As already noted, Knight would like to see an increase in the number of women and minorities on this team. Since the team conducts hundreds of presentations and seminars every year, he has challenged his team to actively recruit women and minorities to try out for the team through those presentations and seminars, as well as "spreading the word" at the various parachute clubs throughout the Army. Recruiting prospective team members to tryouts is no promise they will be selected at the end of those six grueling weeks of continual evaluation and training. Neither Knight nor any commander to follow him can risk lowering team standards by taking substandard jumpers or soldiers onto the team. The American people expect quality, not quantity from the Golden Knights.

IMMUTABLE STANDARDS

During the Grenada Invasion in October 1983, a young paratrooper in the 82d Airborne Division received a hard blow to the side of his head, or at least to the kevlar helmet protecting his head. Hours later he discovered a 7.62 mm slug (fired from a Soviet-made AK-47 rifle) lodged in the side of his helmet. The kevlar material, which is basically a multi-layered fabric compressed together, had stopped the bullet. News about the incident spread among the troops quickly. Not only was the new helmet less heavy and more comfortable than the old "steel pot," it actually did the job it was designed to do—stop small arms fire.

The incident was only briefly mentioned by the press, who were more concerned with the invasion itself than human interest stories from the soldiers involved in that invasion—soldiers who rescued the American medical students who

were the reason for that invasion. Not to let the story die, however, and to ensure confidence in the equipment issued its paratroopers, the 82d Airborne Division now displays that helmet in its museum at Fort Bragg, North Carolina.

A few years ago, the Army reported that a number of kevlar helmets then being sold to it were substandard—not capable of stopping a bullet from a .22 caliber rifle, much less an AK-47. Back at Fort Bragg, troops in the 82d Airborne Division were appalled and angry that an American manufacturer would risk their lives to make a larger profit by taking shortcuts in quality. Each man wondered if the helmet he was wearing was one of the good ones or one of the bad ones, and would his helmet really protect him in combat?

Because a few substandard helmets had gotten into the system, the reputation rightfully earned by the kevlar helmet was seriously compromised.

Confidence in a piece of equipment that had been proven to save lives was now riddled with doubts. Whenever quantity takes priority, quality always suffers. And when quality goes down, with it goes confidence, motivation, initiative—morale. A similar incident in the recent Panama Invasion restored some of the faith in the kevlar helmet, but not necessarily in the procurement system which awards contracts to the lowest bidder. Substandard helmets got through the system once. Are promises alone enough to restore confidence?

At a reunion of special friends held in Fayetteville, North Carolina, December 9, 1989, more than four hundred men and women of diverse backgrounds gathered from around the country. Their ages ranged from 19 to 71. Some never finished high school; others now teach high school. Some were veterans of World War II, others Korea, Vietnam and Grenada.

They were all different, but every one alike for each at one time during their military careers wore the black and gold uniform of the Golden Knights. They made up 30 years of history and not one of them was substandard—not one.

During those last few months preceding the official activation of the Army Parachute Team in 1961, John Hollis says they took a closer look at themselves—soldiers who were about to become the official ambassadors of the U.S. Army. Longevity in the Army was now of great importance. One couldn't very well represent the Army if he was himself in a hurry to leave it. Personal appearance, public speaking skills and military bearing weighed heavily upon the decision of who should stay, who should go and who should be added on. Jumping skills, though less important than soldierly performance, were still a prime consideration. You simply don't put substandard jumpers out over a

crowd of spectators. In short, Hollis says, they were looking to obtain and keep the very best soldiers in the Army at that time.

The "best of the best" is still the Golden Knight standard today. The number of slots needing to be filled each year, and even a desire to increase the number of women on the team are factors considered by tryout cadre, but only after they are satisfied a tryout meets jumping and soldiering standards first.

"We look for team players," said **Staff Sergeant Dave Haberkorn**. "You can be a world class parachutist and an airborne Ranger super hero, but if you aren't willing to work as part of a team, the Golden Knights can't use you."

The screening process for bringing prospective Knights to tryouts is the first step in "weeding out" all the "I'm in it for me" applicants, Haberkorn explained.

A Golden Knight tryout application requires a copy of a

soldier's military records, a full length photo and a letter by that soldier explaining why he or she wants to be a Golden Knight. The records give essential information about that soldier's background such as duty assignments, military and civilian schools attended and scores on physical fitness and skill qualification tests.

The full length photo reveals the wear and fitting of his or her dress green uniform. It also reveals to some extent if that soldier is overweight.

"Appearances are everything on this team," explained **First Sergeant Jeff Moon**. "If a man appears to be fat, as far as the public's concerned, he is fat."

Moon paused, grinning as he explained that the photo is not intended to gauge how "good looking" or how "ugly" an applicant might be. If looks alone were a qualifying factor, Moon says the team's ranks could use some immediate trimming. The photo simply shows whether a soldier has a neat, soldierly appearance.

The most important part of the application is the letter in the applicant's own words. **Staff Sergeant Tom Shrivers** points out the letters aren't "graded" for punctuation, grammar, spelling and style—although a poorly written letter might indicate that soldier is not too concerned with details or clarity. The whole purpose of requiring the letter is to see how well the applicant expresses himself. There's still another use for the letter, however.

"The Golden Knights have a saying," explained former first sergeant, Bobby "Spider" Wrenn. "You can't spell the word 'team' with an 'I.'"

Despite this simple revelation, a number of applications include letters that read something like the following: "I want to be a Golden Knight because I want to do this...and I want to do that...to achieve my own personal glory. Besides, I look good in basic black and gold. And since I am already famous in my own mind, it's only proper that I lend my many talents to this team."

He who would be first will be last. Fortunately for the team and the American public, these "I'm in it for me" applicants never even get an invitation to tryouts. Those who do receive an invitation, come to Fort Bragg for 6 seven-day weeks of continuous training and evaluation—evaluation not only by the cadre, but by their own peers.

Peer reports are done at the end of each week to allow the tryouts to rate each other's performance as team players. A poor rating on a peer report supported by a poor evaluation by the cadre will result in that tryout being cut from the program. By the end of the sixth week, usually half of the tryouts will have been sent back to their units with pointers about how they might improve themselves to prepare for next year's tryouts. But those still remaining aren't secure in being selected.

"If there are 14 slots to be filled, we're not going to keep 14 tryouts just to fill those slots," explained **Sergeant First Class Ben Currin**. "If we only have one woman tryout, we're not going to keep her just because she's the only woman. She has to prove herself just like every other tryout."

"Just because" is not an accepted reason for doing anything in today's Army. Responsibility and authority must be perfectly balanced to accomplish any mission. A leader cannot order a subordinate to do something, then deny him the authority to get it done. Since Golden Knight tryout cadre are tasked to select the best soldiers and freefall parachutists in the Army, it would be senseless to deny them the authority to drop tryouts from the program who don't meet Golden Knight standards.

Taking that concept a step further, today's professional NCOs know that an unlawful order is a senseless order for it is one which simply will not be followed. And as far as the NCOs who make up and run the Army Parachute Team are concerned, lowering team standards to meet quotas of any kind would be "unlawful" because it would lead to the destruction of the Army Parachute Team itself. For that reason, no such order will ever be given by the team commander, the Department of the Army or the Department of Defense.

"If the team has 10 openings to fill, and we only have five tryouts qualified to be on this team, only five tryouts will be selected," Currin said, prophetically. "It's better to have five quality soldiers than 10 mediocre ones. This team can't afford to take anything other than the best."

For three decades, the American people have come to expect the best performers, best competitors and best soldiers to represent them as Golden Knights. Allowing one substandard soldier to wear the black and gold uniform of the United States Army Parachute Team would tarnish its well-earned golden image. Maintaining that image through their immutable standards is therefore the never-ending goal of the Golden Knights.

ABOUT THE AUTHOR

Staff Sergeant Randy C. Murray served in the active Army from 1973-1977 as an indirect fire infantry paratrooper with the 82nd Airborne Division at Ft. Bragg, NC and C Company (Abn) 1 Bn 60th Infantry at Ft. Richardson, AK. He rejoined the Army in 1983 as an infantry paratrooper with the 4th Bn 325th Airborne Battalion Combat Team, 82nd Abn and the United States Army Parachute Team.

During his time of service, Murray has received a multitude of decorations and awards including the National Defense Medal, Good Conduct Medal (3 ea), Army Achievement Medal (2 ea), Army

Commendation Medal, Parachutist Badge, Jungle Expert Badge, Expert Infantryman's Badge and British Jump Wings.

Between his times of service in the Army, Murray attended North Carolina State University and received a bachelor of arts degree in Language, Writing and Editing in 1982. He took second place in the 1986 Chief of Staff Writing Contest. In addition, he has written several articles in various military and civilian newspapers and magazines.

Murray currently serves as Media Relations Director for the U.S. Army Parachute Team (Golden Knights). He is responsible for media coverage for the team's two parachute demonstration teams and two competition teams.

Murray resides in Fayetteville, NC with his wife, Gloria, and their two children, Shelly and Patrick.

INDEX

Abbeville, La., 2575
Abbotsville International Air Show, 61
Adriatic Cup
  1958, 62
  1959, 94
  1963, 58, 62
Air Force (see U.S. Air Force)
Alabama, 5
  Dothan, 155
  Leroy, 191
Alaska, 60
  1967, 60
Albritton, Paul (Private First Class), 73
American Flag, 80, 102, 103, 106, 113, 119, 134, 173
America's Cup Trials (see Australia)
Angel Of Peace Memorial (see West Germany)
Arizona, 54
Arizona State University, 61, 75, 213
  Fiesta Bowl, 61, 75, 146
  Phoenix, 61, 75, 80
  Scottsdale, 75
  Sky Harbor Airport, 146
  Sun Devil Stadium, 145-6
  Yuma, 54, 81
Army Times, 98
Arrellano, Arnold A. (Sergeant), 70
Arrender, Jim, 24, 46, 54, 62, 64
  1960 World Sytle Champion, 62
Arrufat, Fernando, 103
Arvidson, Brad (Sergeant First Class), 157
Australia, 65, 121
  America's Cup Trials, 1986, 61
    Fermantile, 61
  Royal Australian Army Military Nationals, 1989, 61, 65
  Sidney, 61, 121
    Opera House, 61

Bangs, Glenn (Captain), 30, 31, 64, 104, 117, 174, 175, 199
Barbarick, Joseph (Staff Sergeant), 73
Bartow, Aaron, 127, 128
  Dennis, 127
  Dennis II, 127
  Nathan, 127
Beatles, 203
Belcher, Joseph (Staff Sergeant), 6, 73
  Diana, 84
Berry, Albert (Captain), 42
Bishop, Dick (Major, retired), 42
Blue Angels (see U.S. Navy)
Bonds, Marcus (Captain), 136, 189-90, 200-2
Boston, Massachusetts
  Dean Junior College, 149
  Lincoln Sudbury High School, 148
Bourquin, Gerald (Sergeant First Class), 15, 47, 131
Brake, Jack, 64
Brazil, 160-61, 174
Breaux, Kevin (Sergeant), 25-6, 157-58
  Heather, 26
  Ryan, 26
  Stacy, 26
British Parachute Team, Red Devils (see England)
Bronze Star, 192
Brown, Charlie (Staff Sergeant) 28-9, 31, 33, 115, 119
  Bill (Sergeant First Class), 169, 179
  Colin, 127
  Jake (Sergeant), 146, 148, 175
Brydon, Loy (Sergeant), 15, 47, 94, 136
Buckley, Michael (Sergeant), 73
Bulgaria
  Sofia, 33, 46
  5th World Championships (1960), 33, 46
Bullington, Bartley (Staff Sergeant), 73
Bunkhard, Ace, 62
Burma, 44
Bush, President George, 60, 173
Byard, Danny (Sergeant), 15, 45, 47, 94, 131, 189

C-47, 67, 70, 95, 178

C-123, 68, 130
C-130, 5, 121
C-141, (LDC-37), 135, 171
Caribou or CY-7A, 70, 178, 182
California, 46
  Davis, 199
  El Centro, 46,
  Golden Gate Bridge, 61, 163
  NFL Super Bowl, 61
  Pasadena, 61
  Santa Anna, 191
  San Diego, 29, 30
  San Francisco, 61, 163
  Spring Valley, 73
Camp Lejeune (see North Carolina)
Canada, 142
Captain, Janice, 83, 158
Carpenter, (see Iowa)
Charette, Wilfred (Sergeant), 15, 47, 52, 197
Chicago, (see Illinois)
China, 44, 191
China Rifles, 194
Cleveland (see Ohio)
Coffman, Jim (Staff Sergeant), 30-1, 64, 68, 199
Cold War, 54, 65
Collingwood, Chuck, 64
Colorado, 213
Columbus College (see Georgia)
Columbia (see South Carolina)
Congressional Record, 93
Coney Island, (see New York)
Connally, Doreen, 83
Conquistadors, 51
Cotton Bowl (see Texas)
Counseil Internationale du Sport Militare, 4th (CISM), 26
Counsil, Donna, 6, 86
Crane, Joe, 42
Creef, Doug, (Chief Warrant Officer) 174
Currin, Ben (Sergeant First Class), 37-8, 145-48, 156-60, 219
  Lois, 155
  Nancy, 156
  Thomas, 155
Cypress Gardens (see Florida)
Czechoslovakia, 154

D'Agostino, Pete (Chief Warrant Officer), 134, 147
Daley, James (Captain), 66, 75, 146, 178, 180-83
Dandridge (see Tennesee)
Daniel, James R. (Captain), 69
Davenport, Matt, 64
DaVinci, Leonardo, 41
Davis Airfield (see Muskogee Oklahoma)
Davis, Cecil (Staff Sargeant), 73
  Jason (Staff Sargeant), 127, 148, 205, 206
Dayton (see Ohio)
DelConte, Richard (Chief Warrant Officer Three), 73
DeLuca, Ed (Master Sargeant), 69
Denning, Larry (Private First Class), 147
Delta Junior College, 163-64
  Design Group, 164
Department of Defense, 74
DeVault, Mike, 64, 117, 175
Diamond Head State Monument (see Hawaii)
Dominican Republic, 213
Dothan (see Alabama)
DNA molecules, 32
The Drop, 42
Duffy, Ray (Master Sargeant, retired), 22, 26, 40, 53-4, 62, 65, 158, 161-62
Dunaway, George W. (Sargeant Major), 22

Eckbold, Earl (Sergeant First Class), 134
Edge, William (Sergeant First Class), 15, 47
El Salvador, 194
  Army, 194
Engels, Jimmy, 42, 60
England, 65, 174
  Red Devils Parachute Team, 27, 65
English, Alva (Specialist), 94
Europe
  European Command (EUCOM), 94
  Supreme Headquarters Allied Powers Europe (SHAPE), 94

F-4 Phantom Jet, 200, 201
F-27 Fokker, 16, 66, 117, 145, 182, 213
Fairchild Hiller, 68
Fayetteville (see North Carolina)
Federal Aeronautics Association (FAA), 134
Federation Aeronautique Internationale (FAI), 31, 204
Feldt, Elisa, 25-7, 84
Feliciano, Pete, 131
Fernandez, Maurice, 64
Fiesta Bowl (see Arizona)
Finn, Bob (Sergeant First Class), 6, 30-1, 38, 64, 86, 95, 117, 175, 176, 199
Fish, Russell, 80
Florida
  Cypress Gardens, 146
  Gainesville, 61
    Gator Bowl, 61
  Tampa, 191
  Zepherhills, 64, 69, 204
    4th World Parachuting Championship (1981), 171
    Crash January 30, 1968, 69
Folkestad, Eric (Sergeant), 148, 185
Fort Benjamin, Indiana, 199
Fort Benning, Georgia, 46, 192
  Airborne Division, 75, 138, 148, 159
  75th Ranger Battalion, 140, 144
  197th Infantry Brigade, 140
  Officer Candidate School, 175
  Officer Infantry Basic Course, 175
Fort Bragg,, North Carolina, 9, 41, 65, 70, 73, 80, 102, 130, 133, 138, 155, 157, 160, 166, 174-75, 182, 187, 192-93, 203, 213, 216, 218
  XVIII Airborne Corps, 44, 92, 93, 203
    XVIII Airborne Corps Public Affairs, 44
      Office, 44
      Sports Parachute Club, 142, 154
  82nd Airborne Division, 30, 33, 42, 51, 140, 142, 149, 154, 163, 173, 174
    Club, 139, 141, 204
  Camp McCall Airfield, 34
  Iron Mike, 150
  Museum, 173
  Officers Candidate School, 175
Fort Campbell, Kentucky, 162
  101st Airborne Division, 162
Fort Lewis, Washington, 174
  2nd Ranger Battalion, 144
Fort McClellan, Alabama, 203
  307th Army Band, 203
Fort Meade, Maryland, 96
Fort Ord, California, 137
  Continental Army Command, 46-7
Fort Rucker, Alabama, 184
Fort Stewart, Georgia, 174, 175
  24th Infantry Division, 186
Fortenberry, Dick (Specialist Four), 15, 45-7, 54, 63-4, 131
Frannington (see Massachusetts)
France, 33, 52, 62, 93, 161, 174
  International Air Salon, 61
  Laferte-Gaucher, 93
  "Coup deMonde", 1961, 62
  Paris, 61
  Vichy, 65
  World Cup, 1988, 65, 164
"French Cross", 192
French, Mark (Sergeant), 174
Friddle, Bill, 155

Gabriel, Mark, 64, 117, 175
Gaddy, Charlie, 135
Gallagher, Annie (Sergeant), 60, 82
  Mason (Sergeant), 103, 136
Gardner, Alan (Captain), 69
Garnerin, Andre Jaques, 41
Gateway Arch, St. Louis (see Missouri)
Gaven, James (General), 192
Gator Bowl, Gainesville (see Florida)
Georgia, 5, 61
  Stone Mountain, 61
Gerber, Andy (Sergeant First Class), 30-1, 64, 115, 117, 168, 170-72, 175, 199, 204
Germany, 65, 94, 141, 148-49, 154
  West, 26, 137
    Angel of Peace Memorial, 61

Army Parachute Team, 65
  Freemantle, 61
  Stuttgart, 137
  West Berlin, 61
  Special Forces (Europe) Parachute Team, 65
Geyer, Jeff (Staff Sergeant), 179, 185-87
  Reverend Jimmy, 186
  June, 186
Godwin, Bill (Sergeant), 135
Golden Gate Bridge (see California)
Goldie, Dave (Sergeant Major), 6, 95
Gornick, Mike (Chief Warrant Officer), 66, 75, 134,
  146
Grant, Ricardo (Staff Sergeant), 70
Green Beret Club, 141
Green, Gary L. (Sergeant), 70
Greenville (see Pennsylvania)
Greenville (see South Carolina)
Grenada, 60, 61, 144, 152, 213, 216, 217
  St. Georges Island, 61
  Queens Park, 61
Grieves, William (Colonel), 93-4
Guerra, Paul (Sergeant First Class), 136, 143, 145
  Tina, 145

Haberkorn, Dave (Staff Sergeant), 35, 123, 136, 217
Harmon, Dick, 26, 162
Hattisburg (see Mississippi)
Hawaii, 60, 96, 100
  Diamond Head State Monument, 61
  Honolulu, 60, 61
    NFL Pro Bowl, 61, 143, 152
Heegeman, Charles, 64
Heimlich Maneuver, 206
Helicopter
  Blackhawk, 5, 164
  CH-47, 34
  "Huey", 6, 9
  "Husky", 52
Hibbing (see Minnesota)
Hollis, John (Command Sergeant Major), 6, 15, 43, 47,
  51, 58, 69, 131, 178, 190, 197
Honduras, 195
Hope College (see Michigan)
Humphrey Hubert, (Senator),14
Hunt, Elizabeth, (Staff Sergeant), 189

Illinois, 136
  Chicago, 136
India, 44
Indiana, 73, 137
  Fairland, 137
  Notre Dame University, 146
    Marching Band, 146
  Terre Haute, 73, 146
Indo-China Mini War, 10
Indonesia, 175
  Bali, 175
    International Sky Diving Championships, 175
Institute of Heraldry, 51
International Air Salon (see France)
Iowa, 27
  Carpenter, 27
Istel, Jacques, 45, 48, 192
Italy, 45, 188
  Geronimo Sport Parachute Team, 188
  Sicily, 45
  Vincenza, 188

Jackson, Bill (Sergeant), 96, 157-58, 163-65, 199
Jackson, Paul E. (Staff Sergeant), 70
Japan, 188, 191
  Okinawa, 183
Jimenez, Luis R. (Chief Warrant Officer), 183-84
  Candice, 184
  Clay, 184
  Helen, 184
  Marette, 184
  Nanette, 184
John Nichols High School (see New York)
John Wayne Airport, 191
Johnson City (see Tennessee)
Johnson, Tom (Sergeant First Class), 70
Jones, Cliff, 158
  Mark, 158
Jutas, Roger, 103

Kansas, 70, 106
  Kansas City, 106
  Kansas Liberty Memorial, 106
  Overland Park, 67
Kassens, Ken (K.C.), 6, 134-35, 141-43
  Angela, 143
Kauble, Cristy, 83
Kentucky, 81
  National Guard, 81
Kidd, Don (Public Info. Officer) (Sergeant), 6, 10, 46,
  51, 92-3, 106
Kilcline, Thomas J. (Vice Admiral), 74
  Study, 74
Kimbrill, Jeff (Sergeant), 135
Kinser, Raymond (Staff Sergeant), 73
  Kirk, Preston L. (Sergeant), 70
Knight, Bill (Staff Sergeant), 26
Kirk (Lt. Colonel), 81, 134, 178, 188, 212, 215, 216
Korea, 44, 94, 104, 131, 140, 182-83, 217
  7th Infantry Division, 197
  23rd Infantry Regiment, 44
  XVIII Infantry Regiment, 44
  Chosin Reservoir, 192
  Inchon Landing, 192
  Olympics, 1988, 17, 60, 61, 102, 159, 175, 199
  Republic of Korea (ROK), 102, 199
  Seoul, 31, 60, 61, 102, 104, 170
  South Korea, 31, 60, 61, 102, 197
  Veterans, 131, 153, 192
  War, 192
Kryske, Leo N. (Sergeant First Class), 69

Lackey, Chuck (Sergeant), 31, 115, 158-61, 199
  Athlete of the Year, 157
  Charles, 160
  Eric, 160
  Kenda, 160
  Kisti, 160
  Sharon, 160
Lane, Doug (Staff Sergeant), 90, 106, 135
Lasher, Jeanne (Sergeant), 60
Lee, Willie (Sergeant), 31, 64, 169, 176-78, 199
Leibach, Steve (Crew Chief Specialist), 134
Letbetter, Bobby (Specialist Four), 15, 26, 47, 52, 69,
  162
Lewis, Herald "Harry" (Sergeant First Class), 15, 25,
  53
Jim (Sergeant), 26
Lincoln Memorial (see Washington D.C.)
Lorenzo, Todd (Sergeant), 64, 115, 169
Luke, John (Staff Sergeant), 28-9, 134-35, 14

Major League Baseball World Series, 61
Malone, Paul (Major), 189, 209, 210, 211, 212
Martin, Roy (First Lieutenant), 15, 26, 45, 47, 52, 62,
  197
Maryland, 59, 135
  Ocean City, 59, 135
  Williamsport, 30
Mason, Fred, 41
Massachusetts, 22, 51, 54, 73
  Frannington, 73
  Orange, 2, 51, 54
    6th World Championships, 22, 51, 54
Massapequa (see New York)
Mayo, Mike (Sergeant First Class), 6, 15, 26, 31, 62,
  65, 93-4, 131, 209
Michigan, 200
  Hope College, 200
McDonnall, Robert (Private First Class), 15, 20, 47, 52,
  54, 68, 130
MIA/POW, 213
Miller, Phil (Sergeant First Class), 65
Milwaukee (see Wisconsin)
Mississippi, 163, 182
  Drew, 163
  Hattisburg, 182
Missouri, 61, 73
  St.Louis Gateway Arch, 61, 112-13, 123, 163
  Springfield, 73
Mohler, Gary (Sergeant First Class), 108, 157, 214
Moon, Jeff (First Sergeant), 31, 159-60, 186, 188, 190,
  214, 215, 218
Morton, Todd (Specialist), 146
Mosby, John S. (Confederate Colonel), 176
Mount Rushmore (see North Dakota)

Mullins, Charles L. (Captain), 23
Murray, Raymond (Colonel), 192
  Randy, 220
  Gloria, 6, 220
  Patrick, 6, 220
  Shelly, 6, 220
Muskogee (see Oklahoma)
Muzquiz, Fernando (Chief Warrant Officer), 77, 190

National Anthem, 146
Navy (see U.S. Navy)
Needles, Chris (Captain), 62, 70, 74, 151
New Jersey, 73
  Patterson, 200
New, Jim, 190
New Mexico, 170
  Anthony, 170
  Military Institute, 170
  State University, 170
  Silver City, 144, 152
New York, 52, 73, 80, 163, 182
  Brooklyn, 61
  Coney Island 1961, 57, 61
  Lake Placid, 60, 61, 100
  1980 Winter Olympics, 100
  Massapequa, 73
  New York City, 61, 80
  World Trade Center, 61
  Niagara Falls, 61, 119
  State University, 182
  Statue of Liberty, 61, 80, 163
  Yankees, 30
NFL Pro Bowl (see Hawaii)
NFL Super Bowl (see California)
Niagara Falls (see New York)
Nicaragua, 194
  Contra War, 194
  Miskito Indians, 194
Nichols, Nick (Staff Sergeant), 146, 148
Nipper, Jim (Sergeant First Class), 157-58, 166-67
North Carolina, 52, 130, 156, 185
  Camp Lejeune, 173
  Fayetteville, 36, 71, 73, 98, 130, 160, 217
    High School, 59, 203
    Market Square Court House, 98
    Municipal Airport, 75
    Observer, 71
  General Assembly, 73
  Greenville, 156
    State University, 155
  Kittyhawk, 61
    Wright Brothers National Memorial, 61
  Oxford, 155-56
  Raeford, 159, 17
  Raleigh, 67, 135
    WRAL-TV 5, 135
  Silk Hope, Chatham County, 67, 71, 75, 135
  Wilmington, 52, 53, 66, 130
North Dakota, 61, 102, 119, 140, 163
  Key Stone, 61
  Mount Rushmore, 61, 102, 119, 136
Notre Dame University (see Indiana)
Novosel, Michael (Chief Warrant Officer), 131, 178
Nykoping (see Sweden)
Noriega, General, 199

Ocean City (see Maryland)
OH-58 Helicopter (see Helicopter)
Ohio, 50, 136, 180-81
  Cleveland, 50, 205
    Air Show, 205
  Dayton, 50
  Warren. 180-81
Oklahoma, 23, 30, 91, 165, 213
  Muskogee, 23, 30, 91
    Davis Airfield, 165
Oleksy, Kevin (Sergeant), 6, 86, 96
Olympics, 31, 32, 61, 100, 171
  Summer (Seoul, Korea 1988), 31, 32, 61, 171
  XVIII Winter (Lake Placid, NY), 61, 100
Opera House (see Australia)
Orange (see Massachusetts)
Overland Park (see Kansas)
Overmyer, James (Private), 49
Oxford (see New York or North Carolina)

PT-17, 191
Palmer, Ralph (Sergeant First Class), 15, 47
Panama, 193, 199
  A-Team, 193
Pan-Am Games 1987, 138
Parachute Club of America (see U.S. Parachute Club)
Parrish, Edward (Sergeant), 73
Patterson, Fred Jr. (Master Sergeant-retired), 135, 139-40
  Fred III, (Private), 139
Patterson (see New Jersey)
Pawlak, Richard V. (Chief Warrant Officer), 69
Pearson, James (Second Lieutenant), 15, 47, 94
Pease, Rodney (Chief Warrant Officer), 73
Pelter, Joseph (Staff Sergeant), 73
Pennsylvania, 73, 181
  Chester, 198
  Greenville, 181
  Philadelphia, 140
  Radner, 73
  Reading, 174
  Thiel College, 181
    75th Anniv. Army's adoption of the Parachute, 180

  Westchester, 198
    High School, 198
  Pentagon, 163
Perry, "Jim" James (Captain), 6, 9, 14-5, 19, 42-9, 52-5, 93, 131, 190-95, 197
  Laurel, 6, 85-6
Petric, (Captain), 26
Peyton, Kevin, 6, 64, 146, 169,
  Phil (Specialist), 106, 136
Phoenix (see Arizona)
Pope Airforce Base, 182, 212
Presley, Elvis, 203
Pro Bowl (see Hawaii)
Puerto Rico, 184
  San Juan, 184
Purple Heart, 192

Queens Park (see Grenada)

Raeford (see North Carolina)
Radner (see Pennsylvania)
Rafferty, Paul, 64, 115, 169, 199
Raleigh (see North Carolina)
Rhodes, Scott (Staff Sergeant), 64, 115, 169, 172-74
  Tricia, 174
Rice, James (Staff Sergeant), 73
  Pat, 72
Richardson, Alsee (Sergeant First Class), 202
Richister Woodrow L., "Butch" (Chief Warrant Officer), 181-82
Richmond (see Virginia)
Rivera, Ed (Staff Sergeant), 146-48, 152-54
  Anna, 154
  Joshua, 153
Roberts, Clifford (Chuck), (Sergeant), 6, 20, 146-47,
Runnels, Douglas (Second Lieutenant), 15, 47, 53, 130

St. Patricks Day 1958, 45
St. Louis (see Missouri)
Salmans, Gary (Sergeant), 136
Salvador Army, 184
San Juan (see Puerto Rico)
Sanborn, Kew, 45
Sargeant, Don, 46
Saudi Arabia, 174
Schoepple, Clay, 62
Scottsdale (see Arizona)
Sellers, Karen, 80, 82
Sheppard, Merrill (Major), 44, 94
Sherritt, Cathleen (Sergeant), 84, 134,
Shields, Mark (Master Sergeant), 73-4, 104, 148, 150-52
  Linda, 152
Shriver, Tom (Staff Sergeant), 6, 86, 96, 138, 196, 218
Sicily (see Italy)
Silk Hope (see North Carolina)
Silver City (see New Mexico)
Simmons Army Airfield, 66, 74-5, 212
Skydiving and Parachute Magazine, 94
Smith, Roy (Private First Class), 15, 74

Soldiers Magazine, 98
South Carolina, 182
  Columbus, 182
  Greenville, 185
    Christian High School, 185-86
Southeastern Parachute Conference Meet (1972), 64
Soviet Union, 42, 53, 54, 62, 65
Spain, 32, 161, 174, 215
Spann, John (Staff Sergeant), 86
Spring Valley (see Califonia)
Springfield (see Missouri)
Statue of Liberty (see New York)
Stearns, Cheryl, 63-4, 75, 78-80, 87, 158, 211
  Joan, 75, 77
  William, 75, 77
Steele, Jeff (Sergeant), 34, 99, 130, 146, 175
  John (Sergeant), 146, 175
Stillwell, Joseph Jr. (Brigadier General), 3, 10, 15, 19, 43-4, 51, 93, 158, 190, 193-94
  "Vinegar" Joe (father) (Brigadier General), 44
Stewart J.E.B. (General), 44
Stiner, Carl (General), 130
  Liberty Bell Award, 130
Sullivan, Ed (Show), 203
Super Bowl XVII, 104-5, 152
Supreme Headquarters Allied Powers Europe (SHAPE) (see Europe)
Sweden, 159, 161
  Nykoping, 159, 161
  World Parachute Championships, 159, 161
Sweeney, Mike (Sergeant), 105
Switlicks, 191

Tampa (see Florida)
Tennessee, 66
  Appalachian Fair, 143
  Dandridge, 139
  Knoxville, 61
    World Fair, 61
Terre Haute (see Indiana)
Texas, 61
  Cotton Bowl, 61
  Dallas, 61
Thacker, Gene Paul, 53, 62, 157
  Tim, 157
  Tony, 157
Thunderbirds (see U.S. Air Force)
Tivat (see Yugoslavia)
Tulsa (see Oklahoma)
Turkey, 79
  Women's Style and Accuracy Competition, 79
Turner, Bob (Sergeant/Army Photographer), 49, 52-3, 85
  Hank, 148

U.S. Air, 81
U.S. Air Force, 55, 68, 74, 137
  Academy, 201
  Thunderbirds, 23, 28, 30, 68, 151, 162
U.S. Army, 137
  Combat Pictorial Detachment (CPD), 96
  Golden Knights
    Alumni Association, 161, 195
    20th Reunion, 54
  Green Berets, 9, 38, 192
  Rangers, 55
    101st Airborn Division, 55
    20th Reunion, 54
  STRAC (Strategic Army Corps) Sports Parachute Team, 15, 22, 43, 45-6, 93
  XVIII Airborne Corps Artillery, 41, 92-3
    Sports Parachute Club, 26
  77th Special Forces Rigger Detachment, 138
  82nd Airborne Division, 30, 181, 192
  319th Military Intelligence Battalion, 60
U.S. Marine Corps., 43, 173, 191
  U.S. Military Academy, 24, 44, 55, 199
    West Point, 44, 200
U.S. National Sky Diving Championships
  1965, 161, 162
  1977, 77
  1981, 30
  1987, 31
  1988, 31, 160, 165
  1989, 25, 158, 167
U.S. Navy, 54, 55

Blue Angels, 23, 30, 54, 151, 162
U.S. Parachute Association, 56, 169
  Achievement Award, 56

Vanderweg, Phillip J. (Sergeant First Class), 69
Vares, Terry Bennett, 63-4, 79, 82, 158, 212
Venezuela, 53
  Army, 53
  Falcons, 53
Vermont, 59, 107
Vichy (see France)
  World Cup Competition 1988, 65, 159
Vietnam, 69, 131
  Laos, 192
  Mekong Delta, 194
  Operation "White Star", 9, 44, 192-93
  POW-MIA's, 85
  Tet Offensive, 194
  War, 69, 74, 150, 155, 182, 183, 193, 204
Virginia, 28, 46
  Danville, 46
  Richmond, 28
  Thomas Jefferson High School, 28
  Yorktown, 166

Warren (see Ohio), 180-81
Wagner, Chris (Sergeant First Class), 31, 64, 115, 169, 199
Wainer, Harvey (Sergeant), 135
Washington D.C., 42, 61, 69, 123, 134, 151, 213
  Lincoln Memorial, 60, 122, 134
  Presidential Inauguration, 61, 123
  Vietnam Memorial, 69, 213
  White House, 42
Wasley, Michael (Specialist Five), 73
Welch, Francis (Sergeant First Class), 73
Welgos, Tom, (Sergeant First Class), 111, 157
West Chester (see Pennsylvania)
West Point (see U.S. Military Academy), 200, 201
"White Star" (see Vietnam)
Whittle, Chuck (Captain), 95
Wicks, Bruce (Colonel), 182, 190, 198-200
  Kay, 198
  Robin, 198
  Rocky, 198
Williamsport (see Maryland)
Williford, Sherman (Brigadier General), 131, 162
Wilmington (see North Carolina)
Wisconsin, 177
  Milwaukee, 143
  Cedarburg Heights H.S., 143
  City of Festival Parade, 143
  Omro, 177
  Oshkosh, 177
  University, 177
Wolfe, Leon D. (Specialist Four), 70
  Robert (Staff Sergeant), 73
Woman's Army Corps (WACS), 75
World Fair (see Tennessee)
World Trade Center (see New York)
World War II, 92, 93, 131, 183, 191, 217
  Burma, 44
  China, 44
  India, 44
  Pacific Campaign, 92
Wrenn, Bobby "Spider" (Master Sergeant—retired), 6, 59, 140,
150, 190, 202-5, 218
Wright Brothers Memorial (see North Carolina)
World Championships (XI), 31

Yeider, Bill (Sergeant First Class), 195
Yonkers (see New York)
Yorktown (see Virginia)
Yuma (see Arizona)
Yugoslavia, 43, 51, 62
  Adriatic Cup, 1963, 51
  Porto-Roz, 62
  Tivat, 43, 62

Zeigler, Tim A. (Sergeant), 70
Zephyrhills (see Florida)

GLOSSARY

AFF—(Accelerated FreeFall) A parachuting course in which basic freefall instruction is compacted into a few hours of classroom work by a qualified AFF jumpmaster/instructor, followed immediately by 8-10 freefall jumps (depending on student) under the direction of two AFF Instructors. Compare to static line course that requires 15 jumps, the first five of which with a static line.

Altimeter—A device worn by a parachutist that tells him his altitude, whereby he knows when to activate his parachute.

Barrel rolls—Performed by crossing the legs or dropping the arms in such a way as to cause a horizontal roll to either side.

Biplane—Canopy Relative Work maneuver in which two jumpers stack their parachutes. The upper jumper slides down the lower jumper's suspension lines to where he is nearly standing on the lower jumper's shoulders.

Bust—An uncompleted relative work formation usually caused by one jumper attempting to enter the formation too fast.

Cell—A section of a ram air canopy. Air is funneled into these holes, giving lift to the parachute the way an airplane wing gives lift to the plane. Square canopies can have five, seven or nine cells.

C.I.S.M.—(Counseil Internationale du Sport Militaire) an annual all-military sports competition that first included parachuting in 1964.

CMF—(Career Management Field) Military jobs are divided up in categories or specialty fields. For example, there are four types of infantry jobs: 11B light infantry; 11C indirect fire infantry; 11H anti-armor infantry; and 11M mechanized infantry. All four jobs come under CMF 11.

CRW—(Canopy Relative Work) Any maneuver in which two or more parachute canopies are stacked one atop of another. The world record set by the British is 24 canopies. In competition, four jumpers stack their chutes and then rotate vertically with the top jumper, "leap frogging" to the bottom during two minutes working time.

Cutaway—Functionally, it's what a jumper does when his main parachute fails to open properly. He releases or "cuts" it away before activating his reserve to keep the two canopies from entangling. As a maneuver, it is used to show what the jumper would do if an emergency did occur.

DA—Department of the Army.

DoD—Department of Defense.

Exit Point—A point in relation to the ground from which the jumper exits the aircraft. Winds aloft and on the ground are taken into consideration in selecting this point.

FAI—(Federation Aeronautic Internationale) French-based organization governing sport and competition parachuting around the world. Each country has its representative body. In the United States, it is the United States Parachute Association.

Forward or Backward Loops—Performed by arching the body with leg and arm movements similar to that in high diving.

Freefall—Parachuting from an aircraft without any attachment (such as a static line) to aid in the deployment of a parachute. The chute is activated by the jumper, by pulling a ripcord or by throwing out a pilot chute.

Funnel—A busted formation sometimes takes on a funnel shape as the lowered jumpers appear to pull the upper jumpers through a hole in the sky.

Gore—A portion of a panel of a round parachute canopy that has been removed to create an airfoil and permit maneuverability.

Ground Control—The most important job during an aerial demonstration. This individual is not only responsible for setting up the target and wind sock, but coordinating with the act preceding and following your own. He also gives the pilot updated information on wind velocities and other changing conditions on the ground.

HAHO—(High Altitude, High Opening) Military freefall course taught by Special Operations Command that enables special troops to infiltrate behind enemy lines undetected.

HALO—(High Altitude, Low Opening) Also military freefall course taught by Special Operations Command, again allowing for undetected infiltration of enemy territory.

Hot Target—A message from the ground control to the aircraft that the jump site is ready. It is denoted by unfolding the fourth arm of the X-shaped target on the ground and signaled by crossing both arms at the wrists, forming an X.

Leg—Lower part of a person's anatomy, great for standing on in pairs! Also a non-airborne soldier.

License—Permit applied for when a jumper earns a specified number and type of freefall jumps. The U.S. Parachute Association awards parachutist license when a jumper has met the following number of freefall parachute jumps and passed the appropriate written exam: Class A—25. Class B—50. Class C—100. Class D—200.

Maneuver—A parachute or freefall performance practiced and practiced and improved upon until risks are removed or reduced enough so it can be done safely. Not to be confused with stunts.

MOS—(Military Occupational Specialty) The job a soldier is trained to do in the Army. There are hundreds from which to choose, most of which correspond directly to civilian jobs. Combat arms MOS's, however, cannot be compared to anything offered in the civilian work force.

Parachutist—A freefall jumper who performs in aerial demonstrations and competes in parachute competitions, or someone who simply enjoys jumping from perfectly good aircraft.

Paratrooper—A truly military use for the parachute. These soldiers deploy behind enemy lines, or on top of the enemy to seize and hold tactical positions such as airfields until reinforcements arrive.

Pendulum—Three jumpers stack their parachutes, forming a 3-stack formation, then the lower jumper inverts, thus creating a formation with two jumpers stacked over another jumper who is "swinging" upside down.

Pilot Chute—A small parachute usually stored in a jumper's leg pouch. It is thrown forcibly to one side by the jumper when he is ready to activate his main parachute. The pilot chute inflates and pulls the main chute from its container system.

RW—(Raking & weeding if you've gotten on your team leader's nerves, but usually it refers to Relative Work) Parachute competition in which jumpers link together in freefall to form various geometric formations. Each jumper flies his body relative to his fellow jumper in order to build these formations.

Skydiving, Sport or Precision Freefall Parachuting—Controlled freefall parachuting where the jumper uses his body to maintain a stable horizontal position and employs his arms, legs and trunk aerodynamically for gliding and other aerial maneuvers prior to opening his parachute. Civilian jumpers do it for the sport of it. Golden Knights do it because it is their mission (and for the sport of it after duty hours).

SPC—Sport Parachute Club.

SQT—(Skill Qualification Test) A test given annually to every soldier to ensure he or she is knowledgeable in their MOS.

Stabilized Position—Accomplished by arching the back and spreading the arms and legs immediately upon exiting the aircraft in order to maintain the body in a horizontal, face-to-earth controlled position.

Stunts—Risks taken by carnival act jumpers in years past. Not to be confused with aerial maneuvers performed by the U.S. Army Parachute Team. Golden Knights don't do stunts.

Style & Accuracy—Parachute competition consisting of team and individual events for style—a series of loops and turns performed in freefall—and accuracy—attempting to land dead center on a five centimeter disk.

Terminal Velocity—The maximum speed (about 120 mph) that can be reached by a jumper in freefall. It is reached after the 12th second in freefall.

Toad—Term used to describe a jumper with less than 250 freefall jumps and who "flies" less than stable. In some circles the number of jumps needed to leave "toad status" is much higher. As bad as the "toad" label may be, it's far better than being a non-jumper, who's called by many names (none of which are worth noting in this glossary!).

Turns—Performed to the left or right by increasing or decreasing the airfoil through a combination of arm, leg and body movements.

Tracking—Maintaining a direction of flight in freefall toward one predesignated direction. The jumper's body position tends to look like that of a ski jumper with back slightly arched, feet and knees together and arms to his side.

Tri-Plane—One more canopy/jumper than a biplane.

USAPT—(United States Army Parachute Team) The Army's only official aerial demonstration team, known to the world by its official nickname, the **Golden Knights**.

Thirty Years Of Ext

Golden Knights

ARMY

ARMY

ARMY